ETHIOPIA

Prince of Peace

For more information, or to book an event, contact :
(Email prrinceofpeaceaka@gmail.com

Book design by (Prince of Peace)
Cover design by Prince of Peace)
Second: Edition

1 CONTENT

1

2 GOD THE EMPEROR OF ETHIOPIA
2

3 INTERDUCTION
3 - 6

4 THE GOD EMPEROR OF ETHIOPIA
7 – 2 3

5 KING OF GLORY
24 - 52

6 THE BOY WHO WAS A DUKE AT AGE 14
53 - 68

7 THE ROOT OF DAVID AND CHRISTINATY
69 - 81

8 THE LION OF JUDA
82 - 84

9 NOTES
85 - 111

10 BIBLIOGRAPHY
112 - 114

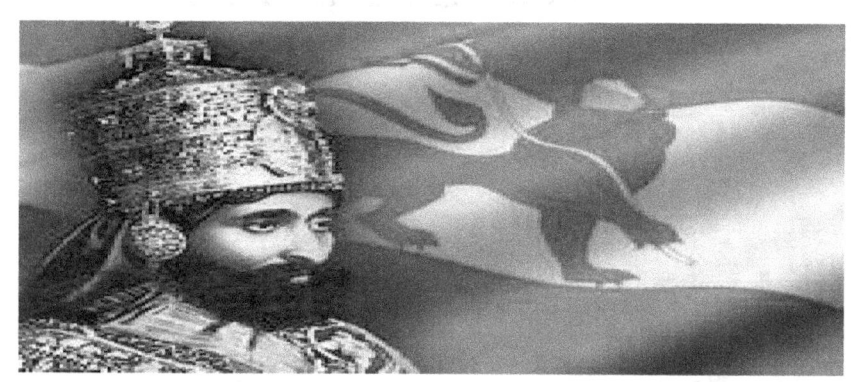

GOD THE EMPEROR OF ETHIOPITA

NTERDUCTION

The history of modern Ethiopia is being compiled by the activities and events that take place each day in the nations supreme, and sustained drive for progress. In all fields as head of state the prime mover and a driving force in this drama, the public utterances of his imperial majesty are in many respects a mirror of these activities, and or the events that determine the course and tempo of Ethiopia's development. On the 75th anniversary of his birth it seems proper and fitting to record some of the most important of these utterances made, on the many occasions that merited public statements from His Majesty the emperor. during his lengthy brilliant and devoted service to his country, and people it is impossible to include all the emperor's pronouncements, in one volume. It is hoped however that through those reproduced herein, the reader will get a fair picture of his majesty's thoughts, and ideas that have provided the centrifugal force of his 37 years, as head of state, and of the preceding years of his early appearance, on the scene as national leader of Ethiopia, these speeches some of them excerpted in the variety of occasions, for which they were intended as well as in the many subjects on which they deal portray the breadth of the emperors vision. They detailed the persistence the determination, and the unflagging drive with which he pursued the application of modern Ethiopian ism, to which history cannot fail to testify. The emperor's idealism coupled with his insistence on transforming his country. Both on the domestic and international fronts, his courage in the face of adversity, his unchallenged perspicacity his keen sense. In evaluating world events his unfailing respect for principles, and his abiding faith in humanity aspects of all of which are found in his public utterances, should make this volume already referenced to certain phases of the history of modern Ethiopia, as the central figure in the Renaissance of the nation after its five years of trials in the late 1930.

INTERDUCTION

his imperial majesty's vital and indispensable leadership has played a distinctive and decisive role. His appearance before the League of Nations and his impassioned plea for justice for Ethiopia, and all small nations, and for international morality remain a classic example. Both breadth of his vision and of a profound comprehension of the foibles of international life subsequently. despite the failure of the League of Nations to live up to its covenant and the gruelling distressed that both the emperor and his country suffered, as a result Ethiopia under his leadership was among the First Nations which at San Francisco in 1945, built the United Nations on the ashes of its predecessor. The defunct League of Nations in these pages will be found expressions of the spirit and the faith that animated the emperor. In this lofty role in international politics his primary motivation that of raising the standard of living of the Ethiopian people, an restoring the ancient stature and glory of his nation runs through the theme of the majority of his public utterances. In them can be clearly seen the inseparable impulse of his whole careers this dedication was amply exposed. As he spoke to his people and the world in the speeches contained in this book, although an ardent reformer emperor Haile Selassie 'I, is no iconic last thus he has advanced the policy of modern Ethiopian ism of philosophy, which he has put into practise from the earliest years of his public careers. The emperor addressing the nation on the 24th anniversary of Ethiopia's victory over aggression. Said Ethiopia is an ancient land, and our civilisation is the result of the harmonious alchemy of the past and the present, and upon which we confidently build for the future. This heritage is the bedrock of modern Ethiopia, in it the people have chosen to distil from the past that which is useful and enduring to adapt those worthwhile attributes of our present-day world, and to fashion this modern Ethiopian ism.

INTERDUCTION

the foundation of our social order, that has served so admirably, the purpose of the nation's steady advance, an absorbing interest in youth has characterised the emperor's entire public careers, Ann is infinitely more than just a formal enlightened paternalism it, is grounded in the fact so frequently expressed by him, that his Ethiopia is built around the future. Haile Selassie 'I, the first will go down in history, as a leader who's concerned for posterity has been both avidin constant. He has always kept close to the people and in particular to the nation's youth, in whom as the speeches herein illustrate, he places immeasurable faith, and confidence. His imperial majesty's constructive influence has been particularly effective in Africa's political emancipation, recalling the days when Africa was a sea of colonialism to the emergence of the organisation of African unity. Haile Selassie 'I, has been both a symbol and a pillar of strength to Africa, as its people fought progressively for their ultimate liberation from colonialism. Today he still stands Foursquare behind the cause of the complete freedom of the continent, in which Ethiopia is the oldest sovereign state. His imperial majesty's faith in divine Providence, is a built-in factor in his personal armoury institutionally, he is defender of the faith, and history will most certainly assess his era. as the one in which the Ethiopian church succeeded. in winning its independence and autonomy after centuries of tutelage under the Alexandrian patriarch shade. in times good or bad the emperors abiding faith in the almighty seems to have been both harbinger an fortress. It being rare for him to make any public utterance without calling on divine guidance and acknowledging publicly, his thanks for God's beneficence minister of state of information.

INTERDUCTION

the selected speeches of his imperial majesty emperor Haile
Selassie I,' the first, one of the emperor's fondest dreams came true
on December 16th, 1961. When he convened at the Haile Selassie
'I, first university in the presence of representatives, from many
world-renowned universities. It was an occasion of pardonable
pride for he had sown the seed and nurtured the plant, that on that
day blossomed into full maturity prior to this event to fill the gap
hundreds of Ethiopians, were sent to institutions of higher
learning abroad a project. That began in the earliest years of his
ascension to the throne in the speeches that follow His Majesty the
emperor deals with the many stages of this development and sets
forth the hopes and aspirations of higher education, in the country
laying foundation stone Haile Selassie 'I, university in the field of
education. We take great pleasure in the fact that the opening of
Ethiopia's first university is near at hand henceforth students who
have demonstrated their capacity and ability, will no longer leave
their homeland to pursue higher education. The university's
faculty is being recruited and its physical plant is being
established. We ourselves have presented our goal an inherited
from our beloved father, as a gift to the nation. To serve as the
nucleus of the university's physical facilities and a formal
ceremony for the handing over of the palace will be held soon. The
population of our capital Addis Ababa have expressed through
their mayor, their desire to erect a monument, to our honour that
they on their own initiative have started raising funds and have
requested that we lay the foundation stone of this memorial today.
It has also been confirmed that the whole people of Ethiopia have
joined hands with the people of Addis Ababa, in this effort, one
higher education, as was indicated on the occasion of our birthday
anniversary on July 23rd.

THE EMPEROR AND GOD OF ETHIOPIA PAGE 1.

We shall now make known to you, our intentions in reference to this monument, we wish first to state, that our heart was touched with our beloved people's desire, to erect in our honour, a statue in recognition of services, which we have rendered to them and to our country. There can be no better way for people to show their deep gratitude to their sovereign, by what means can man's achievements in this world be. Best remembered many people believe that this could be done, by the erection of physical and material structures, others believe that their works are in themselves lasting monuments. We for our part, think that men's contributions which live to influence, the life and progress of posterity are the most permanent monuments, that can ever be erected. It is now 32 years, since we assumed the high service of aiding and guiding the destinies of our people, counting from our Regency when we were destined to the imperial throne of Ethiopia. during this period of our reign a series of problems and trials, have had to be faced. There can be no better testimony to the recognition of our devotion, to the cause of our country and to the welfare of our people entrusted to our care. from the day when we were chosen with the grace of almighty God, the anointed emperor of Ethiopia than this expression of noble sentiments from our beloved and loyal people. We have abiding faith, that the almighty who has vouched saved us, the privilege to reach this present stage, will grant to Ethiopia a bright future, and an enduring destiny. Now when our people are willing to erect a statue, in our image we feel that a duty on our part to consider what would be, the most appropriate means of incorporating in a concrete and lasting manner the sentiments of our people. higher education university a symbol of mutual gratitude, any monument to be left for our people to be permanent must be erected upon spiritual foundations.

it is widely known that during our reign, we spared no effort to promote an extent education and to cultivate the spirit and mind of our people. it is our sincere wish to intimately connect the statue or people intend to erect in our image, and in our honour with a living monument in remembrance of our people's goodwill. Which will go down, in history from generation to generation, linking together perennially the affection of a people to its sovereign our beloved people in contemplating, the erection of a monument in our honour, And we on our part to express our satisfaction an recognise this gratitude have decided, that on the same spot where are people have resolved to build with the funds voluntarily subscribe, the statue to us that a university be erected, and established for the education of Ethiopia's youth. So as to allow them an future generations, to benefit from this happy event, well giving this site for the building and establishment of a university, to represent at the same time a monument to your emperor, for the service and the benefit of your children, and the future generations, and to stand as a symbol of mutual gratitude, between your sovereign and his people. We now lay the foundation stone of the university, the salvation of our country Ethiopia as we have repeatedly stated to you lies primarily in education, as Ethiopia is 1 all Ethiopians are also one, and education is the only way to maintain this condition. higher education you see a opens knowledge paves the way to love, and love in its turn fosters understanding, and leads one along the path of great common achievements. When today is being opened, this University College our feeling of joy has two motivations, or happinesses of two kinds these are private and common happiness shared with many creates a source of permanent affection an understanding. But private happiness is a temporary matter, our endeavour to expand schools has passed from planning to achievement.

Our satisfaction in the field of education is in our days being shared by the Ethiopian people, and particularly by those who have in our profiting by it. Thus, are saying that this would benefit Ethiopia, is now being increased, as has been pointed out by our vice minister work on the university, is progressing rapidly to make successful the work of those educational institutions, of higher education aid of the students and teachers is needed. We hope that the preparation of students and teachers is nearing completion, we are proud to see Ethiopian youth thirsting for learning, although the fruits of education can be applied to evil, as well as to good, things you Ethiopian students, should avoid having a bad reputation can be eager, and energetic in your studies. Be loyal to your country and obedient to your teachers, as Julies an follow truth respect good an beers of good work. February 27th, 1951, agricultural college graduation from the beginnings of recorded history, right up to the Middle Ages, and even as late as the beginning of the industrial age, in which we live agriculture has always been the fundamental source of wealth, for the human race. It gives us immense pleasure to be present here, to inaugurate the College of agriculture, and mechanical arts an occasion which marks a great and far-reaching advance, in our programme for the promotion of agricultural. Education this institution will serve as a source of inspiration, in carrying out the agricultural programme, which we have laid down for the future in establishing this college, for the development of the natural wealth of our country.

Agriculture and animal husbandry on modern, and scientific lines our main purpose, has not been merely to develop an utilised these basic resources to supply the daily needs of our people, but in addition to produce a surplus to be shared with other countries of the world. Ethiopia to some degree has done this in the past, for example when the world was sorely distressed by lack of food immediately after the Second World War, our country although she herself had for five long years been struggling to recover from the terrible damage inflicted upon her, during the war was yet able to perform a significant service, in supplying foodstuffs to the countries of the Middle East. And we have been pleased to observe hell since then our people have increasingly devoted themselves, to improving the agriculture of our country, a country and a people that become self-sufficient by the development of agriculture, can look forward with confidence to the future. Agriculture is not only the chief among those fundamental an ancient task, which have been essential to the survival of mankind, but also ranks first among the prerequisites to industrial, and other developments solid agricultural base history affords us ample evidence, that mankind abandoned its nomadic way of life, and developed a settled communal economy. Only when men became skilled and competent in agricultural techniques, from the beginnings of recorded history right up to the Middle Ages, and even as late as the beginning of the industrial age, in which we now live. Agriculture has always constituted the fundamental source of wealth for humans, only when a solid agricultural base has been laid for our country's commercial, and industrial growth can we ensure the attainment of the ultimate goal, of our development programme.

Namely a high standard of living for our people Commerce, and Industry being concerned in the main with production, and distribution can only develop and profit from existing resources, but cannot create things which did not exist, before most of the districts of our horror province, are populated mainly by nomadic people. Now that we are in a position to anticipate an adequate water supply from the rivers, and wells in the region the area will flourish, and land will no longer life fellow in the province. if only the people of Ogden and all could be educated in agricultural techniques all this can be attained, only by means of the wisdom, which flows from the fountain of education. Well, this college will serve the whole of our country, it's being established in the province of horror is the result of careful planning, and consideration on our part even in this nuclear age. In spite of the revolutionary changes in man's way of life, which science has brought about the problem of further improving, and perfecting agricultural methods continues to hold a position of high priority, for the human race. It is hard to believe that as you stitch it can ever be found, for the occupation of agriculture a sacred task graciously confirmed upon man by God, to serve as the source of his well-being, and the basis of his wealth exchange. Our country Ethiopia, being blessed with an abundance of natural resources need not be anxious about her own needs, however it is our constant endeavour and our firm desire, that our people will produce not only enough to meet their own requirements, but that their production will enable them to share, and exchange the fruits of their labour with other countries. If only Ethiopia with an assured wealth of natural resources, would look at what the Baron Sahara Desert has been made to produce, by the endeavour of trained scientists, she would realise that science is a source of wealth, we would therefore have our students, and scholars accept as their primary duty the attainment of scientific knowledge.

through education, we have placed our trust in this college to be the chief instrument, for the attainment of this high goal. We are confident that the students who have today received their diplomas from our hands, as well as those who follow them in the future will through their achievements furnish us, with tangible evidence of the fulfilment of this our purpose and our desire agriculture, and industry are indispensable. One to the other only close cooperation between these two branches of knowledge, can guarantee the fulfilment of our programme of economic development, for our country. This college which holds a prominent place in the plans, we have laid down for the prosperity and welfare of our beloved people, and country can look forward, to receiving the same constant support, which we have shown in the past. It is with pleasure that we express on this occasion, our gratitude to our great friend the United States of America, for the generous and significant assistance, they have given to this institution as part of their great effort for the development, of the spirit of cooperation an understanding among the nations of the world. We would request His Excellency, the ambassador to convey our thanks to his government, if the late doctor Bennett, who laid the plans for this institution, and whose great desire, and tireless efforts to achieve the establishment, of an agricultural and mechanical College in this country, are well known to us or with us today, to see the fulfilment of his plans how happy he would have been with deep sorrow in our heart, remembering the words men proposes God disposes, we pay a tribute to his memory in this hour. We would like to express our sincere thanks to the director of the programme in this country, the president and staff of this college and, all of our officials who have laboured to bring this institution into being.

It is not enough for the children of Ethiopia, to be recipients of education, they should never forget that the responsibility for passing on this knowledge to others, and of handing it over to the next generation rests on them. January 16th, 1958, engineering college graduation, the existence from ancient times of marvel self-construction among which Ethiopia, probably numbers the monuments at Aksum the remarkable rock churches, and other engineering wonders attest to the long history, of the profession it gives us great pleasure to be present here today. To award degrees to the first graduates of this College of engineering. Which we inaugurated with such high hopes, but a few short years ago this first graduation ceremony marks another step, towards the fulfilment of the goal, which we have set for ourselves and for our country. In our overall programme for the development of Ethiopia, to which we have so long devoted ourselves, when we observe the tangible results produced by our programme, of education to which we have dedicated the major portion, of our time and efforts. It helps us to bear lightly the burden of our labours and provide for us, and for you as well, an occasion for legitimate pride although the first institution, where men received formal training, in engineering was established only a little over 200 years ago. The science of engineering is one of the world's oldest the existence, from ancient times of marvels of construction among which Ethiopia proudly numbers, the monuments at Aksum the remarkable rock churches, and other engineering wonders attests to the long history of the profession. Even in our day engineers are seen constantly adopting, and adapting to their current needs the techniques developed, in those remote times thus fusing the ancient and the modern the old, and the new as you advance in your profession, the value of this combining ancient and modern skills, will become apparent to you, now that your formal education is over you graduate like engineering graduates.

the world over will have to apprentice yourselves, to senior engineers and acquire, the necessary practical experience which one alone can complete, the training which you have received at this college. The degree which you received today, testifies to your growth in knowledge and training, but the measure of your growth in real artists and ship remains to be revealed, in the work which awaits you in your future careers, your success in your profession will not depend on your possession of an engineering degree, it is rather to be judged by the service, you render in future and by the tangible results of your labours having passed, the academic test posed by this college. You now move on to face the more arduous tests posed by life, and the only way to face these tests successfully is to be spiritually prepared for them. Do not make the mistake of assuming that having taken your engineering degree, you can put training and study behind you, and can afford to neglect the acquisition of further knowledge and skill. Man's education never stops and in a profession as complex, and difficult as yours you must strive ceaselessly to put into practise, your theoretical knowledge and to keep yourselves, abreast of new technical developments, If the product of your labours, is not commensurate with the advantages you have received from education your efforts. Thus far will be judged futile, and worthless throughout your life, your metal will be tested by the work you do, and your reputation will depend on the outcome of this test. It is therefore your duty to exercise lifelong vigilance to ensure, that the fruits of your labours are worthy of the effort, spent on your education if you whose minds have been matured by education, and to whom the torch of knowledge has been handed, failed to make a significant contribution to the welfare, of your country. Your responsibility shall be great, indeed in order faithfully to discharge this heavy responsibility, you must be men who love your nation and people.

men of integrity and clear conscience combining patience, and humility be unswerving in your loyalty to your country, which has given you so much into which, so much is do place your faith and trust in almighty God, for without his assistance and guidance, man is but a weak and puny creature. July 17th, 1958, Public health graduation Gondor, when we laid the foundation for the progress, and development of the country, the fact that we granted the constitution was to strengthen unity. So that our country will be built around the idea of 1 emperor Haile Selassie 'I, and one government, in which everyone will be conscious of his duty, based upon the principle of one for all and all for one. We have chosen education as our primary concern, because we believe that it is the instrument, by which our aims could be brought to fruition the spirit of unity within Ethiopia, around 1 emperor, Haile Selassie 'I, the first, emanated from the people of big under and their patriotic efforts have been crowned with laurels. We have made it our constant concern to help them, in their quest for learning for which we have established the various schools, and institutions of learning through education one can keep himself healthy, one can acquire the knowledge of many other things. But without health education and growth of a population, or unattainable, today when we present you with these certificates of accomplishment, our heart overflows with joy, now that you are to begin the medical and health profession. We recommend that you work diligently, for treatment and cure alone is not enough for a country prevention is also necessary. The Amhara race must know that it has an obligation on its part to work in the technical field, no matter at what level to preserve the heritage of one's honour, and culture is praiseworthy, but to exceed the limits may prove detrimental. We have ventured to say this because it has come to our knowledge that there exists here scorned for labour, we have come after having laid the foundation stones for the establishment of a textile factory, a hydroelectric plant and for a bridge, in the development of highways. in order to help in the advancement of the people, of begin Durango jam and less the people benefit through work, our efforts and thoughts will have been in vain, they will have also violated the wish of the almighty, that by ones toil he must earn his living, much cannot be accomplished in the pursuit of spiritual advancement. let alone that of material gains, without labour learn work we have established community education. So that both the youth and the adult may learn education, and the quest for knowledge stop only at the grave. May 18th, 1959, you see a 6th graduation, he who would be a leader must pay the price in self-discipline and moral restraint, this entails the correction and improvement of personal character, the checking of passions and desires and an exemplary control of one's bodily needs, and drives this graduation ceremony is an occasion, not merely for re capitulating and recounting the fruits of past efforts, in terms of examination results and of degrees and diplomas awarded. But also, for fixing one sites upon future accomplishments, obligations and possibilities for the sixth time in the history of this college. We see an imposing group of young men, and women graduate from this institution most of you as in previous years, will continue your studies and prepare yourselves for higher degrees, and varying careers, but whether pursuing further studies, or going directly into the world. All of you will soon be embarking upon a new stage of your lives, we therefore deem it necessary and appropriate on peace occasion, when you have this year's graduating class look back upon your student years, with a measure of nostalgia and look forward perhaps with a measure of understandable apprehension towards your future careers.

to speak to you about leaders and leadership, as you know leadership is required in all fields, and no field is without its usefulness during our visits, however to the educational institutions of our country. We have noticed in answer to our inquiries that the percentage of students, pursuing courses of study useful for the development of technology, and industry has been extremely low. We have therefore council due to take up technological and industrial courses, in preparing for an overall programme the reason for our introducing this topic, at present is that we have found a number of those, receiving degrees. In technological subjects, today to be very small indeed and wish to impresa Panya all that it is our desire, to see a much larger number of our young people, benefiting from the resources. We have on our own and have received, as aid from abroad and graduating in the fields of technology an industrial education. The need for leadership we all know that the need for good leadership, in every walk of life is much greater today, than ever before every aspect of living demands guiding hands, business the professions the Fine Arts. The mechanical arts all and all of you, young people who have been given the enriching opportunity, of an advanced education will in the future be called upon to shoulder ,in varying degrees the responsibilities to leading and serving, the nation it is important however to remember that leadership, does not mean domination the world is always well supplied with people, who wish to rule and dominate others. The true leader is of a different sort he seeks effective activity, which has a truly beneficent purpose he inspires others to follow in his wake, and holding aloft the torch of wisdom leads the way for society to realise, its genuinely great aspirations.

You have learned from your study of history, that the story of nations is often told in terms of the accomplishments, of individuals in every significant. Event in history you will find a courageous and determined leader, and inspiring goal or objective and an adversary who sought to foil his efforts, in any normal society. Everyone has some opportunity to show himself, as a leader even the mechanic, or clerk who has an assistant assigned to him. Not to speak of the doctor with all his helpers, or the officer who commands his troops is a leader within his own sphere. Each has the same opportunities for showing ability, and the same potential satisfactions, as has the leader of a government. The leader is marked out by his individual craftsmanship, his sensibility and inside his initiative an energy, the sense of responsibility leaders are people who raise the standards, by which they judge themselves, and by which they are willing to be judged. The gold chosen, the objective selected the requirements imposed are not merely for their followers alone, they develop with consummate energy and devotion their own skill, and knowledge in order to reach the standards they themselves have said. This wholehearted acceptance of the demands imposed, by ever higher standards is the basis of all human progress, a love of high quality, we must remember is essential in a leader dependability, is another requirement in a leader, to be dependable is to be willing to accept responsibility, and to carry it out faithfully a leader will always be willing to take counsel from his people. but will often have to act on what his own mind tells him is right. This demands that the leader has trained himself, out of any inordinate fear of making mistakes to embark successfully on a career involving leadership demands, A courageous and determined spirit.

once a person has decided upon his life work and is assured that in doing the work for which he is best in doubt, and equipped he is filling a vital need what he then needs his faith, and integrity coupled with a courageous spirit. So that no longer preferring himself to the fulfilment of his task, he may address himself to the problems, he must solve in order to be effective. One mark of the great leader is that he feels sufficiently secure, to devote his thought and attention to the well-being of his subordinates, and the perfection of his task, rather than being constantly worried about the approval or disapproval of others. He who would be a leader must pay the price in self-discipline, and moral restraint, this entails the correction and improvement of personal character. The checking of passions and desires, and an exemplary control of one's bodily needs, and drives leaders have to submit themselves to a stricter self-discipline and develop a more exemplary moral character than is expected of others to be first in place. One must be first in merit as well it should not surprise us, then to find that the greater number of acknowledged leaders, have been people who trained themselves in the art of discipline, and obedience he who has not learned to render prompt, an willing service to others will find it difficult to win and keep the goodwill, and cooperation of his subordinates a leader must stay ahead. Further a leader must possess initiative, which is the creative ability to think in new ways and do new things.

the leader has always to stay ahead, he cannot afford to set up a procedure and then fold his hands, and linger lazily watching it work he cannot be content merely to see nutrients, and take advantage of them he must keep his imagination vividly alive, so as to originate ideas and start trends a word of warning, is in order here to help one subordinates or dependence, at the cost of harm to the public is tantamount to sacrilege, and blasphemy. It is unfortunate that many in positions of leadership, both great and small have been found guilty, of such practises a good leader is devoted to his work and will willingly forgo, even the demands of sleep to see its accomplishment. This does not mean that he is impetuous on the other hand, he maintains a balance between emotional drive and sound thinking, his labours which sometimes appear excessive derived from his firm realisation, that unless a man undertakes more than he can possibly do, he will never be able to do all he can do. It is his enthusiasm that stimulates his energy no matter what our point of departure, in Speaking of leadership we reached the inescapable conclusion, that the art of leadership consists in the ability to make people want to work for you, when they are really under no obligation to do so. The true leader is one who realises by faith, that he is an instrument in the hands of God and dedicates himself to be, a guide and inspire of the nobler sentiments an aspiration of the people. He will kindle interest teach aid correct and inspire those, whom he leads will cooperate with him in maintaining discipline, for the good of the group. He will instruct his followers in the goals towards which to strive, and create in them a sense of mutual effort, for attaining the goal.

basic aspirations to sum up, there is no power on earth in this university or elsewhere that can take a clerk, from his desk or a mechanic from his bench, and easily mould him into a leader to develop oneself one must develop one's own initiative, and perseverance. A man must strive in order to grow, as educated people you will be looked up to, and much will be expected of you will be regarded and rightly. So as those who have the necessary knowledge and the ability to inspire to God, and to lead it is for this reason that we expect from you, to whom we have given the opportunity of education in your chosen fields, great and productive service to our country. These fundamental ideas of which we have briefly spoken this day, constitute we presume part of the thought you have absorbed, during the course of your studies in this University College. May these basic thoughts accompany you during the years ahead and aid you in accomplishing, great things for our beloved country Ethiopia. In conclusion we would like to express our thanks, and appreciation to the members of the faculty and the board of this University College, for their zealous an untiring effort for the growth of knowledge, and the development of character, in the young people who learn here. We would like especially to entrust, our vice Minister of Education based on the statement made by him, regarding the expansion and growth of education in the country, with the high responsibility of assiduously an untiring Lee striving, to carry out the schemes mentioned, and the decisions made, by the board. July 17th, 1959, graduation building college you the students, who leave these holes, today have justified the trust and confidence which your government has reposed in you, in selecting you for attendance at the school from among the many, who have clamoured an who still clamour for the opportunity, to study here in your future work in your daily life, an activities be ever mindful to prove yourselves worthy of trust.

let all that you do, contribute to the ultimate benefit of your motherland, and your fellow men. Let your work always be such that you can take pride in it, and if you do so your country will have reason to be proud of you. Greetings beloved family I am Prince of Peace, and I am very honoured to stand before you, as your host for the enlightening new series speech together, we shall embark on a transformative journey moving into the testament, and profound words of his imperial majesty emperor Haile Selassie 'I. the first, As we embrace the timeless wisdom, that illuminates our part let us unite in this quest for enlightenment and inspiration. for through His Majesty speeches, we shall find solace guidance and a deeper understanding to our ancient royal and priestly heritage. We in Ethiopia have one of the oldest versions of the Bible, but however all diversion maybe, in whatever language it might be written. The word remains one, and the same it transcends all boundaries of empires and all conceptions of race. It is eternal no doubt you all remember reading in the acts of the apostles, of how filibusters the Ethiopian officials he's the first Ethiopian, on record to have followed Christ then from that Leon, what's the word of God has continued to grow in the hearts of Ethiopians. And I might say for myself that from early childhood, I was taught to appreciate the Bible, and my love for it increases, with the passage of time. All through my troubles I have found it, A cause of infinite comfort come on to me, only that labour and are heavy laden. And I will give you rest who can resist an invitation, so full of compassion because of this personal experience, in the goodness of the Bible. I was resolved that all my countrymen, should also share it's great blessing and that by reading the Bible, they should find truth for themselves.

today man sees all his hopes, and aspirations crumbling before him, he is perplexed and knows not the Bible, his drifty but he must realise that the Bible, is his refuge and a rallying point for all, humanity in it, man we'll find the solution of his present difficulties and guidance for his future action, and unless he accepted with a clear conscience, the Bible in its great message, he cannot hope for salvation, for my part I glory in the Bible.

KING OF GLORY PAGE 1.

The man known to history as emperor Haile Selassie 'I, the first, was born on the 23rd of July 1892, in the town of ijaza Goro, not far from the city of Harar in Ethiopia, he was given the name Licht of Arima Conan in his youth, glitch simply means child of well. Tafari means one who is respected or feared, Mekonnen was his father's name Mekonnen and so as he was growing up, he was known as the child of who is greatly respected his father Ross Mekonnen was the governor of the ancient world, city of Harar in eastern Ethiopia, and a key adviser to his near Kingsman. Emperor Menelik II, who was emperor at the time the sleight Harare, Makonnen was born into a significant noble family, which was related to the current imperial dynasty. Through his paternal grandmother, Tafari was descended from the Solomonic, line of kings who had ruled this part of Africa since the 13th century, his mother was Mabbutt Ali, she was the daughter of a ruling chief from willow province to the north, any exploration of the parties life must start by exploring the nature of Ethiopian society, The Empire that ruled it in the late 19th century Ethiopia, and the wider Horn of Africa, have a unique history. 1700 years ago, when the Roman Empire, ruled all North Africa, Roman Egypt emerged as a major early centre of Christianity, in the eastern Mediterranean. Soon the new religion spread beyond the borders of the Roman, Empire down the river Nile and the coast of the Red Sea. It gained many adherents in what Ethiopia is now, which effectively became a Christian country. However, with the Arab conquests of the middle east, and North Africa in the 7th century day. Ethiopia was effectively cut off from the rest, of the Christian world. But it did not convert to Islam, accordingly over the centuries a unique form of Christianity developed here, one which continued to adhere to many of the rights, which were typical of the 4th century church.

Moreover, Ethiopian politics and culture became shrouded in biblical legend, from the 13th century the rulers of the Kingdom of Ethiopia claimed to be descended from the biblical king Solomon. Therefore, their dynastic line has become known as the Solomonic dynasty. This Solomonic dynasty ruled the Kingdom, which centuries ago only constituted part of northern Ethiopia, but between the 13th and 19th centuries it began expanding to the Southwest, and eventually covering an area approximate to modern day. Ethiopia as it did so the Ethiopian empire, became a multicultural state, one which had many different ethnic peoples living under the rule of the emperors. The full most of these were the Oromo and Amhara people, who between them made-up over half the population of the empire. But significant minorities included the Somalis in the far South and east of the country, and the Tigrayans in the northeast, these different ethnicities spoke different languages, and had somewhat different appearances. For instance, the Oromo are a Cushitic people, who dominated the northwestern part of the country, and had been more responsive to the spread of Islam into the region. The Amhara are a semitic people who dominated the Highlands of Ethiopia, and we're much more committed to oriental orthodox Christianity. These ethnic and religious divisions would influence Halie Selassie 'I, rule and indeed the entire history of modern Ethiopia. Indeed, so central are they to the country's history, that the alternative name, which was used for the Ethiopian empire, at the time of Tafari birth was Abyssinia from the Arabic harbour, saw term for mixture a reference to the multicultural nature of the empire. By the mid-19th century, the Ethiopian empire had become one of the most powerful states in Africa, and it needed to be for the great European powers, were entering into a period of accelerated colonisation of the continent to the north Egypt, had effectively become a British protectorate.

And British rule was being extended, down the river Nile into Sudan Ethiopia's western neighbour, and eventually into Uganda and Kenya the southern neighbours of Abyssinia, to the east of Abyssinia along the coastline of the Horn of Africa, a number of European powers acquired territory through treaties, and military intervention in the years leading up to Tafari's birth. The foremost of these was the Kingdom of Italy, which acquired the colonies of Italian Somaliland, and Eritrea in the 1880s, comprising most of the modern day, countries of Eritrea and Somalia the British and French, also carved out small enclaves in northern Somaliland. In the end nearly all of Africa was annexed by the European powers, in what has become known as the scramble for Africa. However, Abyssinia avoided this fate in large part because emperor Menelik II, who came to power in 1889 began a programme of modernisation established at Adis Ababa, as a strong new capital in the centre of the empire, and developed an alliance with the Russian empire, from 1893 onwards through this the Russians sent military advisers, scientists and economists to Abyssinia to advise the country, on how to modernise its government economy, and military with a view to withstanding encroachments by the Italians, British, French, and others. Thus, when Tafari was born in 1892, a new era of Ethiopian history was beginning as a son of a major Ethiopian noble. Tafari was afforded honours from a young age, for instance when he was just thirteen years old, he was given the title of Dej, as match up garden will latter an administrative region near the city of Harar, there just match literally means keeper of the door, and shows that he was a protector of sorts of the region well still barely a teenager. Yet there was little side at this time, that he would ascend to a position of imperial authority, for despite the fact that he was related to the imperial family, and put a menelik II had a clear line of succession in place,

Menelik, as his successor meanwhile Tafari's youth, also saw a concerted effort by the Kingdom of Italy, to connect its two colonies of Eritrea, and Somaliland by conquering Abyssinia in 1895. The Italians invaded Abyssinian, but temperamental aches modernisation efforts proved beneficial, and the short lived first. Italian Ethiopian war ended a year later in 1896, when an Italian invasion force of some 15,000, men were decisively defeated by a much larger Ethiopian army, of upwards of 75,000, at the battle of Adwa, with this Abyssinians independence was secured for a generation in his teenage years. Tafari was promoted further within the empire, in 1907. For instance, he was appointed, as a governor of the province of Sidamo in the South of Ethiopia, beside a daughter during this time the future Princess a row man walks through, the identity of her mother is not entirely certain in 1911. He married Menen in a spell also a member of the imperial family, this was around the time when emperor menelik II, who was nearing his 70th year became increasingly more incapacitated, due to a series of strokes he had suffered eventually died in 1913. Leaving his 18-year-old grandson yes who had found himself increasingly opposed, by the Council of Ministers, which is Grandfather had established, and even by his own aunt malik's younger daughter, Princess Zody to thus when menelik finally died in December 1913. The Council of Ministers and the Princess suppressed news of his passing and did not confirm Yasuo as the new emperor. He was left to enjoy some semblance of power, in the months of followed but his accession would never be proclaimed, and he would never be given an imperial name.

There were multiple reasons, for this opposition to Yasuo firstly in the final year, the young Prince had shown himself disinclined to the kind of administration, and management which was necessary for the ruler, of a rapidly modernising empire. Secondly and more importantly, there were concerns that he was disposed Islam over the Christian faith, which was central to Ethiopian political life. The mid-1910s, they moved to depose him as emperor in the autumn of 1916, he was placed under arrest and would spend the rest of his life, down to the mid-1930s, in detention following his removal from power. So Zody was proclaimed as Empress of Ethiopia. But with the succession now unsure it was decided that her cousin, legit King Tafari in the future emperor Haile Selassie would be appointed, as her Regent and designating successor evidently Tafari tenure as a regional governor of several provinces in the late 1900s, and into the 1910s, had been successful and he had weathered. The political intrigue of the years of Yasser's brief reign very well, the stage was set for Tafari to one day succeed Zody, who was entering her 40s. When she became Empress and did not have any other clear successor. in the years that followed, a clear delineation developed within the government of Abyssinia, between Empress Zewditu and the region Tafari she was a traditionalist, and a conservative ruler while he was following the path Hume, by emperor menelik II in wishing to modernise Ethiopia. In theory the Empress word by far the more powerful figure, but her position was weaker than any of her predecessors as ruler of Abyssinia, for the simple reason that she was a woman in a society which prioritised male rule, as such Tafari was able to claim a great deal, more influence than would have been typical of the power dynamic between them, in most other circumstances both had their factions.

she was favoured by the Ethiopian church, which look kindly on her conservative values on King Tafari, was supported by a clear majority of the Council of Ministers, eventually during the 1920s, emerged as the more powerful figure, and long before her rule would end. Zodi to had begun to withdraw from government and allowed King Tafari, to continue his modernization efforts in the 1920s. The modernisation programme, which was implemented in the 1920s, was multifaceted much of it centred on trying to modernise the government, and administration of Abyssinia, to make it more like those of the European powers. There was a precedent for this, the non-European power which had modernised most effectively in the 19th century, was the empire of Japan it had done so by adopting western methods, and adverse resisted western encroachments, and established itself as a major power itself in the Far East by the 1920s. Abyssinia aimed to at least partially emulate this approach, thus a western style government was established by Tafari one with ministers responsible for individual aspects of governance, in tandem there was a move away from the feudal nature of Ethiopian government, to a political system, where individuals were promoted based on their abilities, rather than their noble rank. Finally adverse India applied for membership, in the newly established League of Nations, a full runner of the United Nations it became a member in 1923. one of the few non Western nations, to ever become a member of the league, even more significant were the attempted economic and social reforms, which were introduced during the reign of Empress Zhou, and the Regency of King Tafari already the first electricity grids, had been introduced to Addis Ababa in the mid-1910s. And this was expanded outwards, in the 1920s.

at the same time efforts, were initiated to begin linking the main cities with roads and eventually railway lies the Telegraph, and other communication systems, which had become commonplace in the western world in the second half of the 19th century. Also finally arrived at Abyssinia or be it in a limited fashion, the National Bank of Ethiopia, was founded in 1927 to bolster the economy and excessive lending rates, were prohibited. Most importantly the judicial system, was overhauled with the fitter Negus law code, a legal system which had been used in Ethiopia for centuries, and which imposed brutal punishments for moderate crimes, such as the loss of a hand for being found guilty of theft, was gradually phased out in favour of a western judicial system, based on elements of the civil and common law. But there was a major backward element to Abyssinian society, which remained slavery was still widespread here. A century after it had been prohibited throughout much of the western world, tokenistic efforts were made to end this in the 1920s as the Western powers criticised the retention of the system in Ethiopia. But Tafari was unwilling to commit to any major efforts, to eliminate it from Abyssinian society at this time meanwhile, Tafari's international reputation was growing. And by the end of the 1920s, he was increasingly viewed as the face of Abyssinia, on the world stage rather than the Empress. Much of this was owing to numerous trips abroad, and state visits. for instance, in 1924 he undertook a tour of numerous foreign capitals, and major cities with other members of the extended imperial family, and the government this was a fact-finding mission, as much as anything else is Tafari at others sought to gain, from direct experience of the western societies. They were attempting to emulate the Abyssinian delegation, with its ostentatious displays of wealth, and court ritual made a significant impression in London and Paris.

King Tafari met King George, the fifth and the French Prime Minister, way more Poincare another significant goal of this foreign tour. Was to try to convince the British and French governments, to provide Abyssinia with access to the Red Sea, by surrendering some territory, in its colonial enclaves in Somaliland elsewhere in the Middle East, and North Africa. Tafari was greeted warmly as the Albert head of state, of virtually the only African nation which had withstood, European colonisation in the 19 centuries. All of this ensured that before he would ever become emperor King Tafari was well established on the international stage, by 1928. King Tafari's position at home in Abyssinia, was such that the Empress could not, but promote him ever further but this time he had monopolised power, within the Council of Ministers. And more importantly, had also moved to secure the loyalty of the heads of the military, and police forces thus on the 7th of October 1928, he was crowned as Nagast and Abyssinian title equivalent to a king. Though still below that of emperor or Empress this replaced his earlier, on horrific of frass which had signified his position, within the imperial line. In the months that followed tensions began, to brew between the emphasis faction, and that of Tafari ultimately culminating in January 1930, in the outbreak of a borderline civil war between Tafari and Wella the emphasis husband, he not only wished to reassert his wife's authority within the empire. But now had designs of replacing Tafari as the head of the government, and having himself crowned as emperor, as rebellion culminated in a major meeting of his horses. And the supporters of Tafari at the battle Adwa of an him on the 31st of March 1930, but with their superior western armaments and methods which included the use of modern aircraft tamari supporters quickly defeated groups as well as army. he himself was killed in the fighting, then in a seemingly unconnected development the Empress died of natural causes.

just two days later clearing the way for Tafari, to claim absolute power in Abyssinia, after years of dual rule between him and the Empress, the mourning period of over half a year, was imposed following the passing of Empress Zhou. But at last, on the 2nd of November 1930, Tafari was proclaimed as the new emperor of Abyssinia, and crowned that same day at the cathedral of Saint George in Addis Ababa, emissaries from many Western nations attended the event and Tafari, featured on the cover of Time magazine. November he also adopted a new name and title the title he obtained was now Neguse Nagas, the king of kings, while his imperial name would be Haile Selassie, Haile means power of Trinity. So, the name Haile Selassie 'I, effectively means the power of the Trinity, however as we will see later the former name, he bore for much of the 1920s. King Tafari was to gain currency again in later years and become increasingly, well-known globally. in the early 1930s, just after his accession as emperor Haile Selassie I the first, the new ruler of Ethiopia quickly oversaw the introduction of Ethiopia's, first modern constitution in 1931. This provided for the establishment, of a bicameral legislature with a parliament at an upper House of Lords, with whom the emperor would share power. It was also intended that a new constitution would further lead to the end of the fetter, Negus Nagas legal system and its replacement, with a western judicial code. The first years of Haile Selassie 'I, reign as emperor, were marked by his efforts to continue and expand, the modernisation programme he had first initiated as Regent in the 1920, however a shadow was increasingly hanging over Ethiopia back, in 1922.

The Italian government, heard being taken over by the national fascist party, led by Benito Salini, after the infamous March on Rome by 30,000, paramilitary fascist black shirts one of Mussolini's, great desires was to build Italy into a great power again and to resurrect the empire; Italians had enjoyed back in the days of Rome 2 millennia, earlier to that end in the 1920s, he had engaged in a series of aggressive actions initiating, A brutal war of conquest in Lija, which had been a nominal colony of Italy's since 1912. As well as bombing the island of Corfu, during a dispute with the Kingdom of Greece annexing the city, of humour in what is now Croatia and establishing, a protectorate over Albania, through a series of treaties in the mid-1920s. With these advances made in the early 1930s, Mussolini's attentions turned to the Horn of Africa where he increasingly, wishes to correct what he deemed to be an historical failing of Italy's, its loss to Ethiopia. In the first Italo Ethiopian all back in the 1890s, if Abyssinia could be conquered, it would also make a continuous colony of Italy's lands in Eritrea, Ethiopia and Italian, Somaliland in turn making it the predominant colonial power, in the Horn of Africa in 1934, tensions between Haile Selassie 'I, government, on the Italian colonial administration. In Eritrea and Somaliland began to flare over long running boundary dispute, which had been caused by Italy's wish to build a railway line, through the region connecting it to divided colonies, which Ethiopia was in the middle of this had culminated, in Italy building a military Fort but well in eastern Ethiopia in December 1934. The Italian presence here was challenged by Halie Selassie' 'I, government, when Abyssinian troops were sent to war on the 5th of December, this led to violent engagements between the Italians and The Ethiopians, resulting in dozens of deaths on both sides, an international diplomatic standoff followed known as the Abyssinia crisis in early January 1935.

Haile Selassie 'I, government, protested to the League of Nations, months of diplomatic toing and froing would follow. But essentially the British and French governments, who are best placed to act as intermediaries were unwilling, to block Italian aggression at a time when they were trying, to win over Mussolini as an ally in Europe. In the face of the rise of the Nazis, following Adolf Hitler's, seizure of power in Germany in 1933, consequently while negotiations followed for months it eventually became clear to Haile Selassie 'I government, that the Italians were intent on using the well incident in December 1934, on the ensuing diplomatic standoff, as an excuse to declare war on Abyssinia, and that the League of Nations, was not going to take any effective measures to try to stop Mussolini's aggression, The second Italo Abyssinian war commenced on the 3rd, of October 1935, when the Italian general Emilio de bono crossed over the border, from Italy's colony of Eritrea into northern, Ethiopia with 10s of thousands of Italian troops. There was no formal declaration of war, this was to be one of the most significant conflicts globally. During the winter war period, between the First World War, and the Second World War, eventually involving hundreds of thousands of troops, and personnel on both sides. It would last for just over a half a year, the sides were evenly matched throughout. Though while The Ethiopians, were numerically superior despite the best efforts to modernise their army, since the 1890s their forces were still resoundingly based on mass infantry divisions for instance, Haile Selassie' I, government had just a handful of tanks. The Ethiopian Air Force, consisted of little more than a dozen planes by way of contrast with Haile Selassie 'I, government, was eventually able to deploy hundreds of tanks in East Africa, as well as massive artillery barrages and a significant Air Force presence. Thus, while the Italian army, would be shown in later years, to be enormously deficient in European.

The war, which was initiated in the autumn of 1935, was clearly a David versus Goliath type conflict, in which the Italians had the upper hand, in a way which they had not back in 1895. When the first Italo Ethiopian, war was launched response to the invasion of Abyssinia, the League of Nations sanctioned Italy on the 7th, of October 1935, four days after the initial incursion by de Bono's troops. The two primary countries, within the league to whom the responsibility fell for challenging. The Italian government's, actions were Britain and France, who were the foremost colonial powers across the African continent, and who had colonies nearby themselves in Somaliland, and across Ethiopia's western, and southern borders in Sudan and Kenya. In the case of Britain yet while the conservative LED national government, of Stanley Baldwin in Britain campaigned, on and won an election in November 1935, on the premise of supporting the League of Nations, and its mission here the desire to appease. Italy and prevent it from drifting closer to Nazi Germany, was paramount and the whole of al packed details of which, were leaked by the British press in early December, effectively outlined a plan whereby Abyssinia, would lose roughly half of its territory to Italy allowing the Italians, to connect their colonies of Eritrea and Somaliland. This was completely unacceptable, to Haile Selassie 'I, government, and a complete betrayal of the mandate of the League of Nations. Outrage followed hall resigned, as British foreign minister and ultimately the revelation, of details of the pact ended any efforts, to find a diplomatic solution to the conflict. The whole of al pact and the wider Abyssinia, crisis is generally seen as also sounding, the death knell of the League of Nations, an institution which had now conclusively proven its inability, to prevent aggressive nations, like Italy and the empire of Japan, from invading its enemies with no justification.

Italy and Japan, with the termination of diplomatic negotiations in December 1935. The war intensified on the ground, in Abyssinia, by now the Ethiopian government, was preparing for its own counter offensive against, the Italian incursion in the north. This was led by Haile Selassie 'I, the Emperor Selassie 'I, in person, and had hoped to sever the Italian lines, of communication and launch a counter invasion, of Eritrea initially admit with considerable success. But in the early months of 1936, the tide turned once general Pietro budo Leo, who had previously overseen the Italian campaign in Libya, was appointed as governor of Eritrea, and the leader of the military, effort in succession to Debono whose oversight, of the invasion had been deemed too cautious by Mussolini, by olio initiated a brutal campaign, in January 1936. In which poison gas was widely used, against the Ethiopian armies, through these methods a series of victories were quickly won by bad olio at the battles, of Tambien amber Adam Ann Shearer in northern Ethiopia. In the late winter and early spring of 1936, a final effort to maintain the northern front by, Emperor Haili Selassie 'I, the first, was defeated at the battle of macho on the 31st of March 1936. Following which northern Ethiopia was effectively under Italian control, on the 26th of April 1936. But olio launched what he termed, the march of the iron will a swift dry southward from the northern front, around Essien wallow province towards the Abyssinian capital of Addis Ababa, some 200 kilometres. The campaign was accompanied, by much fanfare and propaganda, in the fascist, media back home in Italy. A large, mechanised column was the centrepiece of this drive with over 2000 tanks, cars and other vehicles. Included in the operation which transported some 12,500, Italian troops, speedily towards Haile Selassie 'I, capital.

by now the Ethiopian armies, were decimated from the northern offensive, and as the Italians neared Addis Ababa, in early May the emperor and his family fled from the capital, and made their way towards the border, with French Somaliland crossing over. As the Emperor, went into what would be years, of exile from his realm, three days later at roughly 4:00 PM, on the afternoon of the 5th, of May 1936. But olio arrived in Addis Ababa, at the front of a column of 1700 vehicles. In the hours that followed Italian troops began entering the city, in what was more of a procession than an actual siege, and occupied prominent, all over the capital. The war was now effectively over the second Italo Ethiopian war, came to an end in May 1936, with the fall of Addis Ababa. And the flight of emperor highly Selassie 'I, from Ethiopia, however pockets of resistance remained particularly in the South, and West of the country which were still unoccupied, by any Italian forces accordingly fighting would continue, for months and years to come. Indeed, all our senior, was never actually brought under effective Italian control. Yet from May 1936, the Italian government, claimed to have won the war, as such the new colony of Italian Ethiopia, was declared to be in existence, by Mussolini on the 9th of May 1936. However, this was soon annexed into the newly proclaimed, colony of Italian East Africa, which incorporated Abyssinia, Eritrea and Italian Somaliland and which stretched all the way across, the Horn of Africa completing the ambition for Italy to create, a contentious colony here 40 years after it had first been, attempted in the mid-1890s. Here the Italians would impose A brutal form, of colonial governance following many of the quasi genocidal, policies which have been developed in Libya, in the 1920s of confining thousands of people to concentration camps and favouring a divide, and rule policy whereby the different ethnic peoples of Ethiopia, were pitted against each other with the Italians.

now largely in control of his country, Emperor Haile Selassie 'I, made his way to Europe, his first mission was to present Abyssinia's, case at the League of Nations in Geneva. However, his timing was far from propitious in Europe, Nazi Germany had initiated an aggressive programme, of military rearmament in 1935, and in the spring of 1936, while His Majesty was fighting in northern Ethiopia, Hitler had ordered his troops into the Rhineland of western Germany, which German troops had been prevented from entering, under the terms of the Treaty of Versailles. The treaty that brought the First World War to an end. Consequently, the governments of Britain and France, were no more willing to adopt an aggressive, stance against Italy in 1936. Then they had been the previous autumn, nevertheless while his efforts had redressed were in vain, the emperor gained acclaim for a speech he made at a meeting of the league, on the 12th of May 1936, in the course of which he denounced, the rise of fascism and the use of poison gas by the Italian. The emperor was subsequently named time magazine's, man of the year but the result for Ethiopia, was the same the league was unwilling to take concerted action against Italy, which in any event withdrew from membership of it in December 1937. Meanwhile the Emperor headed for England, where he would live in exile throughout the late 1930s, while he was in exile in England, the world's politics was in continual flux Germany, aggression intensified in 1938, with the annexation of Austria, and then Czechoslovakia. In 1939 when the Nazis invaded Poland, the following September Britain and France, declared war triggering the start of the Second, World War. For the time being Mussolini adopted, a cautious stance and did not enter the war, but when the Germans undertook a blistering military campaign, in the summer of 1940, that effectively brought continental, Western Europe under Berlin's control.

The Italians decided to side with Hitler, declaring war on Britain and France, on the 10th of June 1940, and invading southeastern France to acquire territory. There what this now meant was that the Italians, and the British would square off to each other in East Africa, on the 13th of June 1940, and Italian air raid was launched against British, Kenya in the first action of the East Africa campaign. This was all part of a wider Italian initiative to conquer Britain's, colonies in each shipped and Sudan and thus unite Italian East Africa. With Italy's growing expanse of territory in North Africa, at first these campaigns preceded well from Mussolini. But by early 1941, the weaknesses of the Italian military were becoming wholly apparent, early in 1941 with Italian operations, in the Sahara Desert faltering Mussolini, called on Hitler for aid, a German Expeditionary force the famous Africa core led by Erin Romo, was dispatched to North Africa that March. But there would be no major military support, offered to the Italian position in East Africa. Thus, in the course of 1941, the British gradually turned the tide here, and began pushing the Italians back into Ethiopia, and Eritrea after their initial advances into Sudan and Kenya. By this time the emperor had left Britain, and had returned to the Horn of Africa, to oversee parts of the campaign to reclaim his homeland from the Italians. The emperor himself the fighting here was undertaken, by a broad mix of British Ethiopian Eritrean, free French and free Belgian forces, crucially they had naval superiority, and by early 1941, a new front was being opened in Eritrea. Following a naval operation in the Red Sea, as a result by the late spring of 1941, the Italian defence was collapsing on all fronts, as the troops in East Africa found themselves, effectively cut off from major reinforcement by Mussolini's government.

Finally on the 5th of May 1941, in an event which was stage managed to occur exactly five years, after bud olio had arrived with his Italian forces to Addis Ababa. The emperor re-entered the capital of Ethiopia, and proclaimed the liberation of the country, from Italy, the restoration of the Solomonic dynasty. The emperor Haile Selassie 'I, to power in Ethiopia carried a proviso from the British, who had largely restored the emperor to power, slavery had to be banned entirely in Ethiopia. There had been piece meal efforts at doing so, as far back as the 1850s, at which time Britain was using its influence as the global superpower, of the 19th century to try to curb the slave trade across Africa. These had intensified under emperor menelik II, and during Haile Selassie 'I, time as Regent back in the 1920s. But slavery had never fully been eradicated in Ethiopia and was still a feature of Ethiopian society when the second, Italo Ethiopian war was initiated in 1935. Following the conquest, the Italians, had declared the abolition of slavery, A paradoxically humanitarian act for a state. Which elsewhere in Africa was engaging, in genocide and whose German allies would soon be using, the slave labour of millions of Jews, poles, Czechs, Russians and other subject peoples across central and Eastern Europe, to drive its war economy. The British government made it clear to the emperor, that this abolition needed to continue, once he was restored to power, and that he would have to take concerted steps, to make a reality of that abolition. A decree was issued by the emperor, to that effect in 1942, from which date we might say that slavery, was finally abolished in Ethiopia. Though the East Africa campaign had resulted in a significant victory, for the allies in 1941, it took four more years for the Second World War, to end in the defeat of Nazi Germany, and its allies. Then it did the League of Nations, was succeeded by the United Nations, which Ethiopia became a charter member of in 1948.

Emperor Haile Selassie 'I the first, had gained favourable consideration for his nation, when it came to the settlement of East Africa in the aftermath of the conflict, when the Ogden region was granted to Ethiopia. A region which had long been disputed, by the Italians British and Abyssinia, prior to the war, the emperor main concern during these years, was to continue the modernization of his country, considerable strides had been made in doing so, in the 1920s and 1930s. But there were still deeply entrenched best interests in the country, within the nobility and the church which were resistant to too much change, occurring too rapidly His Majesty the emperor, was determined to accelerate the pace of change as the war came to an end, in the mid-1940s. Eventually this would result in 1955, with a revised constitution which moved beyond the constitution of 1931, and incorporated elements of the US constitution. However, in practise, the election of parliamentary delegates remained, in the hands of the nobility and other powerful bodies and Ethiopia, certainly did not become a western style democracy, under His Majesty the emperor rule. In the post war years many controversial issues, began to arise in Ethiopia in the post war period particularly. So, during the 1950s one of these concerned, one of the former Italian colonies Eritrea this small northern neighbour of Ethiopia's, had been placed under British administration. Following the conclusion of the East Africa campaign in 1941, in the aftermath of the war the allied powers were in favour of Ethiopia's, claims to Eritrea though a small section of the West of the colony, was to be joined to British Sudan, accordingly when British rule of Eritrea came to an end in the early 1950s. The country was joined, with Ethiopia but this was to be a federal union, in which Eritrea retained its own identity, and had certain devolved powers held in the hands of its own government.

His Majesty the emperor, though was determined to bring Eritrea which provided Ethiopia, with access to the Red Sea under greater centralised control to this end in 1962. The emperor, he dissolved the independent Eritrean parliament, and annexed the country by that time the Eritrean Liberation Front, or elf an independence movement had launched, an armed struggle against Ethiopian rule. The Eritrean war of independence would continue, for the next 30 years, with the conflict becoming a front, in the Cold War. As the elf another independence movements, drifted into the Soviet bloc to acquire military aid, from the USSR Cuba and others the Eritrean war of independence, was not the only conflict. Which the emperor His Majesty Haile Selassie 'I, the first, government faced ethnic tensions were also becoming more severe in the 1950s, and 1960s. Ethiopia is a nation with approximately 80 different ethnic groups. The empire had effectively been formed through conquest, over several centuries and this had resulted, in many ethnic groups remaining UN reconciled to the dominance of Ethiopia. Above all by the Oromo and Amhara peoples, who made-up over half of the country's population, the emperor Haile Selassie 'I, himself was of Oromo dissent the solution, which was favoured by His Majesty the emperor. And the Ethiopian government, to this situation in the post war period was to foster the concept of ethnic federalism, whereby Ethiopia was divided into over a dozen major provinces, in which different ethnicities predominated. However rather than fixing the ethnic problem, this fuelled it ensuring that many Oromo Amhara Tigrayans Somalis, and others continue to shape, their identity around their ethnicities rather than, their shared identity as Ethiopians. This was already causing unrest in the country, during the emperor reign.

but as we will see this has been compounded, in more recent times of all the ethnic peoples of Ethiopia, those who were most antagonistic to the government, were the Tigrayans who constituted A sizeable proportion, of the overall population roughly 7 or 8% and were, the dominant people in Tigray province in the north of the country. The antipathy of Haile Selassie the emperor government, towards the Tigrayans was clear, for all to see in the 1950s, as the imperial government, persistently neglected the province despite mounting, evidence of pressure on its resources and the possibility, of famine as a result of the destruction of crops by locusts drought, and disease outbreaks of smallpox typhus and other high mortality illnesses, 20 greats eventually did enter farming in 1958. The central government in Addis Ababa did very little, to try to relieve the situation leading to 10s of thousands of deaths. There after a more concerted effort was made in 1959, to address the situation with the emperor Selassie I government, being provided with considerable aid from the administration, of U.S. President Dwight Eisenhower. Nevertheless, by the time the worst of the famine, subsided in 1961 it is estimated that about 100,000 people had died, in Tigray and surrounding regions. While renewed famine struck northern Ethiopia again, in the mid-1960s while the emperor Selassie 'I, reign was increasingly being blackened, by controversies at home including famine in Tigray, a war of independence in Eritrea, and ethnic tensions within Ethiopia. The emperor Selassie 'I, and by extension Ethiopia continued to hold a position, of considerable international respect, as one of the world's longest serving heads of state. He was usually afforded a position of considerable, pre-eminence at major international events, such as the funeral of President John F Kennedy, in Washington DC in 1963. and the former French President, shoulder goal in France in 1970.

Ethiopia also supplied peace, contingents to many areas of conflict such as the Congo in the early 1960s and became a prominent nation within the nonaligned movement of nations. Which were not members of either NATO, or the Warsaw Pact that respective military alliances, of the United States and the Soviet Union, in the Cold War perhaps, most significant of all in terms of international diplomacy. At this time was the emperor Haile Selassie 'I, leading role in the establishment of the organisation, of African unity in 1963. The forerunner of the African Union, the headquarters of the organisation of African unity, was in Addis Ababa, for many years under His Majesty the emperor Selassie 'I rule. Not only did cell as he continued to enjoy, a vaunted reputation on the international stage, in the second iteration of his reign, after the Second World War. But he was viewed by many as, a messianic character in the 1930s, and your quasi religion and social movement, emerged in parts of Africa and the Caribbean. One which mixed elements of the back to Africa, movement which proclaimed that people of African descent, in the Americas would wish to return to the African continent. Now that slavery was at an end and Ethiopian, ism a branch of Christian worship which had arisen in the late 19th century, amongst African Christians. One which looked to the Ethiopian church, as a native Christian Church within Africa, rather than having African Christians, take their directives from European, religious leaders in Rome Canterbury, or elsewhere. This new movement combined specific belief in elements of biblical, theology and a wide array of different social beliefs, he took its name from the emperor His Majesty Selassie 'I, region title dating from the 1920s, King Rastafari thus the new religion, was known as Rastafarianism, and proponents of it viewed His Majesty the emperor as a Messiah.

His Majesty is second coming of Christ, these views must be understood considering Ethiopia's, position as the only African state which resisted colonial conquest. In the 19th century the emperor, did not explicitly seek to be recognised, as a messianic character within Rastafarianism, but he also did not attempt to refute efforts to exalt him in this way. thus, as Rastafarianism gained in popularity in the 1950s, in countries like Jamaica. His Majesty took on an unusual significance, for many people who had never been anywhere near Ethiopia, in contrast to the view of him within Rastafarianism, as a quasi-messianic figure. Haile Selassie the emperor, saw the development of elements of a police state in the country, there were reasons for the Emperor the King of Kings increasing concern about, the security, of his position in 1960, while the emperor was on a state visit to Brazil, elements from the kabure sub agma, the imperial bodyguard had attempted A coup de tar back in Ethiopia, led by the Brothers Grimm Anna, and mango stone airway the insurrectionist's had proclaimed, His Majesty the emperor Selassie 'I son and heir, the Crown Prince as far wasn't as the new emperor, the Prince appears to have been held captive. But how complicit he might have been, in the coup attempt, remains unclear to this day, in any event after four days of violence in and around Addis Ababa, in mid-December resulting in over 300 deaths. The attempted overthrow of the emperor had been suppressed and the leaders were killed. Nevertheless the 1960 attempted coup was significant, in the development of a more repressive authoritarian regime in Ethiopia, under His Majesty the emperor Selassie 'I, in the 1960s, and into the 1970s hand in hand with the development, of this more authoritarian streak in Ethiopian politics. Was a growing disdain for human rights, in the country in the 1960s as student protest movements emerged.

and as communism gained favour in some circles, so as his regime dealt ever more frequently, in mass arrests on the disappearance of political opponents. The press was widely censored and intimidation of groups which questioned, the emperor Haile Selassie 'I, and the government, was widespread by the 1960s, compounding matters, was the war in Eritrea. Where the imperial Ethiopian army was engaging in civilian atrocities, by the late 1960s, for instance in December 1970, 800 civilians were killed by the emperor force, when they attacked the village of honour. Moreover, that has a more in July 1967, 170 men were killed by Ethiopian soldiers admittedly, some of these atrocities appear not to have been state ordered. But the war in Eritrea, was ultimately of the emperor Haile Selassie 'I, making unsurprisingly by the early 1970s. Despite the general positive view of the emperor Selassie 'I, internationally civil rights groups. Such as Freedom House, He still garnered support, amongst traditional groups such as the church, and the nobility who had much to lose, if the old imperial order was overthrown. But many others had no affinity for the ancient ruling dynasty, this disaffection was further compounded in 1972, but the onset of and use of ear famine in Ethiopia. This time it was centred on wallow province, in the north of the country near tiger, this was brought on by drought, and was compounded by an inadequate government, responding to the crisis in the country, the emperor done is best according to the famine in the country, His Majesty the emperor reach out with a heart of love toward is country.

The adjoining regions in the course of 1972, and 1973 while the competition for resource is exacerbated, ethnic tensions here between groups. Such as the Oromos of us answer mollies what was worse news, soon spread that at the height of the famine foodstuffs which were, being successfully produced in wallow were being exported, out of the region to Addis Ababa, and other parts of Ethiopia. Eventually the unrest at Haile Selassie 'I, reign began to boil over perhaps, this was unsurprising in 1972 as famine was gripping wallow. The emperor had turned 80 years of age, he had been in power, in one form or another for over half a century or be it as Regent for the 1st 10 or so years. And with hiatus between 1936, and 1941, the first signs of disturbance, arose in January 1974, when Garrison soldiers in the town, of nigella Borana mutiny over lack of clean drinking water, and poor paying conditions in a symbolic gesture. They detained one of their commanding officers, general did acid do ballet and make show of him having to drink the water, he was forced to consume this resonated with many across Ethiopia. who were disgruntled at the rigid social structure, which prevailed in the country. And the perception of there being an elite of individuals, who are connected to the emperor Selassie 'I, regime in early February, as news of the mutiny spread protests, and insurrection airy movements developed across the country. Crucially, many elements within the military and the police, services joined the disturbances this ordeal for the emperor Selassie 'I whose grip on power, like any author Ethiopia ruler, could only be maintained. so long as the military and security forces remained, loyal by early March so the emperor was under sufficient pressure, that he made several announcements that political concessions, would be made to make ministers and senior government, officials more accountable to the parliament.

Moreover the 1955 constitution, would be re-evaluated to see how Ethiopia's, politics could be made more inclusive, of different groups within the empire. Yet these compromises failed to stem the tide of unrest, instead labour unions called for general strike action, across the country in March 1974, and early in April. The significant Muslim minority in the country, began agitating for greater religious freedoms, by that time elements of the military were evidently in charge, of much of the running of the government. And the emperor Haile Selassie 'I, was losing control of the situation. however, it was not until June, that the infamous DRC was set up this was officially, known as the provisional military administrative council, and consisted of the relatively low-ranking army officers, and officials who effectively seized power, in the summer of 1974. That summer they began a campaign of arrests of prominent political figures and issued a manifesto of proposed reforms finally on the 12th, of September 19 74, years after he first became emperor and nearly six decades, since his accession to a position of pre-eminence in Ethiopian politics. The DRG deposed emperor Haile Selassie 'I, following his deposition Haile Selassie 'I, was placed on the House arrest, his son Crown Prince Asfaw worsen who had been proclaimed as emperor, by the leaders of the failed coup of 1960. Was now again proclaimed by the DRC he was not in Ethiopia at the time, and agreed that his father's deposition, and the actions of the provisional, military administrative council, in proclaiming him as emperor, were illegitimate, accordingly in March 1975. The DRG abolished the Ethiopian monarchy altogether, bringing the empire to an end, and ushering in the creation of a new Ethiopian state. Meanwhile the new military Commanda, had spent much of the winter of 1974, and the spring of 1975, overseeing the execution of hundreds of those who were associated, with the old imperial regime this included some collateral members of the imperial family.

notably Eskinder a grandson of Sir Selassie, who had also been a prominent figure within the Ethiopian Navy. Ethiopia had descended into a long civil war, from which it would not emerge until the early 1990s. The DRC established Ethiopia as a Soviet aligned country, espousing Marxist Leninist principles in the mid-1970s. It was opposed by rival revolutionary groups, such as the Ethiopian people's revolutionary party, and the Tigray People's Liberation front compounding matters, was the ongoing war of independence in Eritrea. And from 1977, onwards a further regional conflict as Ethiopia found itself, at war with Somalia over possession of the province of Ogden, in this morass of political conflicts political violence amplified across the country. With 10s of thousands being killed, in the red terror unleashed by the dreg regime, in the second half of the 1970s by the 1980s, the Ethiopian civil war was made even more traumatic, by the arrival of new famines. The biggest wave coming between 1980, and 1985, in which upwards of half a million people perished. The fighting only eventually came to a conclusion in 1991, once the collapse of the Soviet Union ended. The flow of weaponry, into the Horn of Africa by the time it ended, nearly one and a half million people, had died from the combined effect of military conflict, disease and famine the end of the Ethiopian, civil war in 1991 brought about a brief rest bite from the countries, woes a new constitution was established in the mid-1990s. While Eritrea finally gained its independence after three decades, of fighting there were then efforts to create an ethnos territorial federal state. Where different ethnic groups had control, over different provinces of the country, where they were dominant. However renewed problems soon arose, a new war erupted with Eritrea in 1998, the initial fighting ceased in 2000. But border tensions and intermittent conflict, have remained A perennial problem, in northern Ethiopia.

internally Ethiopia's efforts to resolve, its ethnic tensions. by creating a federal state have largely failed. The governments antagonism, towards the Tigray minority in northern Ethiopia. Which is a deep-rooted legacy of His Majesty the emperor, time as emperor has come to international attention, in recent years in 2020 the Ethiopian federal government, effectively initiated a war against Tigray. One which is ongoing as of late 2022, and which has resulted in war crimes mass famine, and behaviour by the government, which many international observers see as genocidal. While Ethiopia is viewed as having, the potential to become a major economic, and political power in East Africa. As Africa experiences considerable, economic expansion in the 21st century, the structural problems of the country, which were left unresolved. But exacerbated remain a grave problem, in the Horn of Africa and providing the emperor His Majesty Haile Selassie 'I, the first. The emperor was a paradoxical character in 20th century, history on the one hand in the first half of his reign. He made major advances in modernising Ethiopia, even before he became emperor himself, while in the 1930s, he emerged as a figurehead in opposition to the rise of fascism, and brutality as the Italians invaded, and conquered his nation. This reputation as a leading statesman, was cemented in the aftermath of the Second World War. When he forged an independent stance, on the world stage. And was also well regarded for his suppression, of slavery in Ethiopia. Overlying all of this, is the most unusual position which he has acquired as a Messiah, manic character within Rastafarianism. King of kings, Lord of Lords, conquering lion of the tribe of Judah, and elect of God, and light of the world, is imperial majesty Haile Selassie I, the first, these were the titles bestowed on Rastafari Makonnen when he was crowned emperor of the Ethiopian empire, on the 2nd of November 1930, as leader of a civilization had lasted for over 3000 years.

the new emperor would now be seen by millions, around the world as a universal symbol of African pride, and sovereignty at a time when virtually all indigenous, African kingdoms had fallen under European subjugation. And over the course of his 44-year reign, as emperor Haile Selassie 'I, would be many things to many people, to some on electoral Messiah, and God Incarnate, paradoxes and contradictions may be common to all major historical figures. But not many mixed oil and water, quite like the last emperor, of the Ethiopian empire. There's a well-known Ethiopian folk tale, which tells of how to find his father, Ross McCannon governor of the Ethiopian, province of Harar was visited one day by hermit, who came to deliver prophecy fighting alongside his cousin and permanently, Haile Selassie 'I, had played a leading role, at the famous battle of Odwa. In which its European forces defeated Italy, in a raging battle which would ultimately secure Ethiopia, status as one of only two African countries, to have never been colonised. But despite his great military successes and political achievements. The emperor beloved wife had been having serious troubles, with childbearing and had suffered a series of miscarriages, according to the folk tale. However the emperor troubles were finally resolved, when the hermits delivered to him the following prophecy, this time the child your wife is pregnant, with will come into the world, in the best of health and survive, he will grow up to be a fine boy, and when he is still a young man, he would rise to become ruler of Ethiopia, and govern the whole country, with a firm hand. He will restore greatness and pride upon Ethiopia. too many stories about the later empire, with or not the events described happened, will forever remain a mystery, putting aside questions of factual accuracy, the Hermes prophecy from this mystical origin story, provides an almost perfect summary of the complicated life, and legacy of one of the most consequential leaders in modern African history, born to a noble family in eastern Ethiopia. Tafari Mackenna was surrounded by privilege and prestige from the very, earliest years of his life through his mother's bloodline, the very laid claim to Ethiopia Solomonic dynasty. Which according to traditional beliefs had ruled the empire, from as far back as the year 980 BC, according to an ancient tax known as the Cabernet gassed, which is translated as the glory of kings.

The Solomonic dynasty, began when McKay to the queen of Sheba, travelled from Ethiopia to visit Israel's king Solomon, the son of David. Although this famous meeting between the two monarchs, is reference in both the old and new testaments, of the Christian Bible. The Cameron aghast goes into more detail, telling of how the queen fell pregnant shortly, after meeting king Solomon and, subsequently gave birth to his son menelik, the first. Who ultimately became, the first Solomonic emperor of Ethiopia, is privilege of bringing our noble blood, notwithstanding define MacKinnon's childhood was not necessarily, an easy one The young Tafari would gain a first rate, education in power politics and develop a unique blend of charm, peaceful and calm, which would ultimately see him rise to the very, top of Ethiopian society standing at just over 5 foot, all the fairy MacKinnon's was noticeably shorter than most Ethiopian nobles. But what he lacked in physicality, he more than made-up for in charisma, and ambition. just ate 13 Tafari had been appointed, titular governor of Sally, and by the age of 18 he assumed control, of his late father's former province of horror, and just six years later at the tender age of 24, he became the most powerful man in Ethiopia, in all but name when he was appointed, as Ethiopia's imperial Regent. But the fairies rise to power, would be just as much a result of good fortune, as it was due to its political genius. You see just around the same time, as the Far East coming of age, the ruling implemented II, had fallen seriously ill and was under pressure, to choose a successor out of all the Empress, potential as the only two reasonable options in his opinion, where his grandson Legia, so annex eldest daughter, ways arrows are detailed in June 1908, implement Alex offered a severe stroke, and fearing abandoned death announced Legia Sue's chosen successor.

but duty as his young age, Tamper requested the elder statement around this amounted you be appointed, as region planning potential until Leia', who was ordered off to govern. However not too long after his appointment, as Regent rests Emma suddenly died after also suffering a stroke, although many leg was still alive at this point, he was now slowly drifting away, on his deathbed. It was here that the young Leia Aasu, decided to seize his opportunity define senior members, of the imperial court. Leia so refused to share power or agreed to the appointment of a new Regent. And so, at just 14 years of age, he also became the empire's de facto ruler for obvious reasons, he has his power grab would prove to be very unpopular amongst Ethiopia's, appointed as a regions and heir to the throne. what followed would be 14 years of strife political manoeuvring, and blisses in which he also loyalists would unsuccessfully attempt to regain the throne, and a fallout between the more progressive Rastafari, and the traditionalist Empress auditor, would result in a failed attempt to overthrow Tafari as Regent. But after all was said and done and the dust settled, Tafari Makonnen ultimately emerged victorious. This campaign for ultimate power, began with him forcing the Empress Auki the second to crown him king in October 1928, and fallen Empress Auki to sudden death. Two years later the Tafari was finally crowned the Negus Nagas, meaning the king of kings of the Ethiopian empire, from his coronation onwards Tafari, would now be addressed as his imperial majesty emperor Haile Selassie I, the 1st. But unbeknown to the newly crowned emperor, news of his coronation would quickly see him become the central figure of a new religion birth on a land far away, from the boundaries of his Kingdom, on a small British colony where black bodies had long been subject to scorn, and ridicule and subjugation, the news of the emperor coronation would now be seen by thousands of black Jamaicans, as a sign that the day of salvation was at hand.

For, what, was happening in the rest of the continent for many years, the emperor could not trust anybody else, he himself was Minister of Education, he was really very special God person. The story of Ethiopia's great monarch modernizer, and tragic hero emperor Halie Selassie I, starts in the 1000-year-old city of Harare. It was here in Harare the trust of the emperor, as he was known before his coronation, as emperor cut his political teeth, it also serves as a strong symbol of the difference, between the ancient. But primitive feudal society, he grew up in and the modern nation, he wanted to build as a UNESCO World Heritage site, Harare cannot construct new buildings, within the old city's walls, but new buildings do go up outside the old city, and technology creeps in from all directions. So, the coming year is holding you are, I mean like hopeful, no water no problems, Jeff Pierce is a Canadian author, who has spent 10 years, working on a book about the country's war with Italy. In his decade of research, he has interviewed some of the top experts, on Ethiopian history. Emperor Haile Selassie 'I, of course he had a special connection to rare and he invested in coffee plantations. He was very shrewd financially, but he was also very politically astute, disorders of king house the emperor. So sudden medals which, I've gotten from different countries highlight, Joshua is a tour guide who has taught himself, languages and shows visitors around Haile Selassie I honeymoon palace, in his very young the heads last his time actually, I was like too young for that, and my family is used to mention that is one of a good leader, and everything is the main reason what they mentioned is everything is very peaceful, and most of the things are very cheap. They have been brought together by the King of Kings who tried to bring together, his nation his continent, and the world often with his own personal touch.

the most unique a habitable king Haile Selassie 'I, he is a divine king and always stay in the palace, so my mother used to tell me that the emperor always go to a place where people get sick, like in the hospitals and visit people, and people who don't have finance their supported by king Haile Selassie I. So, he's a really nice king in my opinion, King Rastafari was the son of nobleman Ras Mackenna, a provincial governor. He was also an Ethiopian hero for fighting off invading, Italians in the late 1800s Proxima Conan is buried in this hardware church, in a place of honour his compatriots who died repelling the Europeans are buried underneath the church. His father decided to educate young rasta far with tutors of different speciality's, one and Ethiopian monk and the other a Mexican surgeon, Ras Mackenna had two sons upon his death in 1908, his eldest yeller inherited the post two years later, he also passed away. And Rastafari became governor while still a teenager, if you want to understand the Ethiopian, sora feudal politics, is it was really like Game of Thrones. It really was imagining this boy who's a Duke, and he is given responsibilities to run this province at 14 years old, and he's trained by a Catholic priest, he's not trained by an orthodox Ethiopian, cleric so already the other nobles are suspicious of this kid at 24. He was appointed Regent by Empress body, who used the young man to solidify her own hold on power, due to his influential family. This made Rastafari heir to the throne, but he would have to survive some challenges, to become emperor.

When there was a rebellion against him, sometime around when he was Regent and soon to become emperor, he was a fan of flight and he got a plane, and they bombed the machine gun the rebels. So, you had these guys with Spears. and antique rifles and Shields coming out and here's, his plane coming over dropping Bom. Well, that ends that eventually the emperor passed on, and it was time for him to take the throne. This moved him from air through the Ethiopian countryside, to the new capital of Addis Ababa. At that time, we couldn't assume the building, these hearts different kinds of hearts and a very big. maybe one commander of the army, the other low-level commanders they built their hearts around, his around 11,000 people in our server friend. There is no wrote is he, and nobody can assume that therefore, when it is less, he came to the power very big building, this world churches, and this was still primitive. The new emperor had big plans, and decided to build a world class palace, that would impress Ethiopians and foreign visitors alike. This palace also, it was built after his coronation nineteen 74th 1934 with 800 workers and eight months second his palace is now part of a museum, on the ground of the country's first university, which he himself founded 2nd visits with students showed the early priority, was putting on modernising education in Ethiopia. Haile Selassie, I visit many schools throughout all Ethiopia, the emperor was encouraging students to learn, he was even giving us incentives by giving the large amount of money. His Majesty the king, used to give a sweets, and so forth so he was in quite encouraging us to learn, and grow up in sort of his family. Haile Selassie, I wanted young people who could do more than just read or write, who would become diplomats', scientists' engineers, but he had to start with the basics. I think I must have been seven, or eight years old and we lined, up to meet him and that's the first time, I saw him, and he gave us $50 each and I value that money, that's the money I used to buy the first pencil first writing pod.

The young Emperor passion for education, would eventually bear fruit, but in the early years it was opposed, by the nobility the trust his father had come from used to give gifts on Christmas Day. The students going to school today's, the feudal system in the well they call them now, reactionaries but there truly conservative people. I don't want this child to be going to school, and at contaminated by western culture, but never lost his desperate love for people, or his administration for his services. And even the children there is also this is the settlements, children that they sent to school, and his first ministers were composed of mostly comments, not from their ability to push forward, his agenda for modern education. The emperor needed to win over, this nobility which he did by supporting tradition is a very good diplomat, he was also conservative, he tried to keep the condition of Ethiopian, people and the tradition of the monarchy, to keep his hierarchy and he tried to keep the struggle, to unify the country and have everyone support his modern ideas. His Majesty the king, would need to earn the loyalty of those from the countries other 80 tribes, if I list it there are 83 groups, whose represent it is really Italy groups. But asking directly from three Italy cruise, Amara or over on braggy or therefore, but it's not easy groups that have their own culture just tradition, is their belief even their traditional, kings they have it perhaps the most crucial factor, that helped the emperor to unify the country, and gain acceptance for his modernization programme. Was the support of the powerful Ethiopian Orthodox Church, his coronation he was renamed Haile Selassie I the first, in the Amharic language power of the Trinity as emperor he became the head of the Orthodox Church, and by tradition had the religious right to rule. Before 1974 AD, religion it was linked, by the church that's why I said, it's the churches because the churches, it was belonging to for the king, is more prominent king, and I have a power also.

One side of the land for the churches, of course for us, you know we think His majesty the king, like God, you know and the emperor himself, did not give us that going, is abandoned his treasurer who goes out and hunts quid, and our eyes are with him. You know a very short fellow, walking and you know that Negus Nagas, which mean king of kings, that's it you know you can imagine, as that age, he was promoting an agenda based on logic and progressive ideas, legend was a powerful tool of the church, it claims a biblical relationship between its monarch, and the famous Jewish leader and legendary, Wiseman king Solomon, the Ethiopian royal line. So, emperor Haile Selassie I, himself is said to descend directly from the queen of Sheba, I listen as he was in direct, descendant entrance, lest say and queen Sheba, and king Solomon. But we simply took it for granted formula, and respecting perhaps Haile Selassie I, it was before Christ 955 AD, and while she was travelled to trial, which was beautiful woman and glad, she came to be pregnant. And for 9 Months and five days, while Emperor Haile Selassie I, disavowed the legend to educated friends and foreigners. It was part of the powerful hold he had over the common people, the emperor's religious authority would seem to make it easy to unify the nation, but he decided to use his personal touch, to make people believe in his love, for his country. And its people everywhere have car, sometimes helicopter, for example, he was with Kenyans obvious in Glenda tera. Even they are camping and wonder city, where almost 40 kilometres from Adis Ababa, but then you never know his accessibility, also showed he had an open mind, something that helped him learn from his people, and change with the times.

The emperor spent a lot of time, cultivating popularity with his Ethiopian subjects, he also quoted international favour, he was a famous diplomat, and a lot of countries had a very good relationship with him. African countries, Europe or so America whose everyone almost won 2600 something, 1007 times he was visiting 14 progresses during his time, at the province visiting 167 countries in the world. Occasionally there was criticism, what is detracted from say is going there to have fun. But I am sure this for diplomatic purposes, that he went huge go to America meet President Kennedy, or a I don't know. But I think he had much to them both yeah, I don't think he would just type, and come back he would come with programmes, of aid and projects one sort of our or another. The emperor learned about modern ideas, and technology, bringing home worldly knowledge and friendships. Haile Selassie I, anticipated globalisation, even on the modest scale of the 1930s, in 1923, he signed Ethiopia up to be the first African country, to join the League of Nations. The forefather of the United Nations, I decided to come I said this on the course of my people, before the council of the League of Nations. I hope that the council will be good enough to excuse me, from reading the old, related nation, the emperor saw his country, being pulled between the development of an industrialised Europe, and its place in its own still wild continent of Africa. His Majesty the King would send young Ethiopians very talented young, intelligent off to the capitals of Europe, to get an education. 'Because he recognised that the country had to modernise, his initial choice appeared to be to lean toward Europe, there he minds ideas that would help build ministries, schools and institutions, that were aimed at taking Ethiopia from a primitive feudal state to a modern nation. In 1931 he became the first absolute ruler, to voluntarily write a constitution which established A judicial system, while keeping most of the power of government, in the emperor's hands.

1974 His Majesty the king, showed different kinds of developments in the country. We couldn't deny these kinds of changes, in the first the constitution. The Constitution is also improved by his power, time he tried to bring it back to civilization socialise. The society but how far he tried to bring this country. It is it has its own limitations, and splashing was highly interested to have many models, score Arsene to apply for changes to bring fundamental change. In terms of civilization and development, as well his early efforts to modernise, his country through education had only six years to progress, before tragedy struck. In **1936** fascist Italy decided once again, to be the first European colonisers of Ethiopia, the entire world was fascinated, by this war was on the New York Times. It was in the London times **20,000,** black Americans were marching, in Harlem over this war, their battleships in the Mediterranean Sea, in about to go to war with Italy. Over this war and it was a precursor, to the Second World War had a huge impact on world events. The emperor tried to use his connections to head off the Italian attack, His Majesty the king, delivered an impassioned speech, to the League of Nations, pleading for the world's interference of fascists in the gallery did, not stop him. I am here to claim justice Rastafari said, what replies shall I take back to my people, so that the emperor it is us today, it will be you tomorrow. Haile Selassie I the first, said to them it is we today and you tomorrow, after which all the Europeans are falling under the strongest in brutal fiddler, so it was a kind of prophesise, thoroughly taken place. His eloquence moral authority, and logic fell on deaf ears, despite the league's refusal to intervene, he continued to hope that the strength of his people, and the righteousness of their position, would defeat the Italians.

King Rastafari I, stated that it is good that you are here, record this video of me in my palace garden, at Addis Ababa. People who see this throughout the world, is that in the 20th century with first tried and it just cause David will still beat the Italians, had he his youthful stronghold, Mussolini's planes bombed this city, they wiped out the oldest mosque in Africa, and few people know about it. But there were no military installations here, they just decided let's scare the living daylights out of the Harare, and emperor Haile Selassie I, of course he had a special connection, to Harare and he was very hurts. But you know he was very emotionally moved by the plight of the people here. Eventually the Italians took the capital burning his palace, and shocking Ethiopians with their targets, they killed more than 300, the Italians under Mussolini massacred an entire generation, that could have led this country into the 20th, and 21st century. The emperor went into exile in bath England in 1936, I believe it affected his character deeply that he was never going to give up control, and never going to dye vest control to other people, for five long years the emperor was in tough conditions, until 1941. The Italians were chased out by Ethiopian freedom fighters, operating from the countryside, he was welcomed home to reclaim his throne, and once again tried to unite and modernise Ethiopia. But the most difficult time with him with Italian invasion, for example if you've had never been invade by any enemy, is it always free freedom fighter and, it is people defended their country. Five years with his time and he was lucky enough to regain their freedom, and helps many of the African nations, to get their freedom to. And so, it was really very special God person, but his time away from home had given him some valuable perspective, and Haile Selassie I, the first, he would return with a plan on how to build a new Ethiopia, and how to try and empower Africa, so it could look after its own.

the pillars, Haile Selassie I, would build his modern Ethiopia on would be people educators cultural heroes' diplomats, engineers and mechanics, and even pilots to try and connect Africans. He would build an airline and use his wisdom, charm and diplomatic experience, to move Africa forward toward an independence, and unity after independence, the emperor, he really wanted to modernise, this nation, when the EU was established in 1963, and black and white television was introduced, for the first time. So, it's a very exciting time rollers to visit the palace, here in front populous worship, Haile Selassie I, never lost his drive to modernise Ethiopia, restarted with urgency after the Italian occupation ended. And he was back in Addis Ababa, emperor 'Haile Selassie I, the first, order of business was to create an educated class, of young people who could power his country forward, with their intelligence and ability to adapt to new ideas in a rapidly developing world. His Majesty the King, he started with two schools, one for secondary students, and one for university pupils make education his priority, as a battle for many years. all today there are hundreds of secondary schools throughout the nation, and over 150 colleges or universities. So, this is really something that different subject, His Majesty was always interested in help people, and education His Majesty the king, he the Minister of Education himself, to educate all of us to bring us to this level. The emperor took his crusade to create a brilliant team of young achievers, helped steer his nation to where it is now. Modern education is his legacy, the other thing is that not just education but excellence, in education he quickly grew local educators to replace foreigners, and here was a place to start his plan. African leadership in 1958, he invited 200 African students to Ethiopia to study at Haile Selassie I, university.

His Majesty university, now called Addis Ababa university, he wished to transfer his dream of modern education, to the rest of Africa. But he also saw the need to engage, others to promote Ethiopia's role on the continent, by bringing European diplomats' scholars and tourists to Ethiopia. He also saw a way to increase his countrymen's exposure to new ideas, and develop international trade partners, but he needed to make sure they appreciated, his nation this is your personal message. So, His Majesty the king, he turned to some of the young Ethiopians, he was building his contemporary society on including, physic science and technology, many days the emperor king, he was very kind with me, the emperor sent him off to Germany, on Ethiopian Airlines first flight. There he came back with some ideas, on tourism that was the first engager flight, it's your picture for their lives to Frankfurt big deal and in the process the Germans, were talking about tourism, one of his diplomat instructed him, to get a tourism operation going there, His Majesty said to his servant, but set you have to do this job, and set replies, your majesty the king, I know nothing about this job, the emperor told me plain, let the water remember pain, 2nd order so I said OK. Listen His Majesty the king, was always helpful in the efforts to impress, foreigners' dignitaries or ordinary tourists. But whether I tell my Polish which I'll bring them, I bring 105030 tourists to the king, he orders champagne, he orders tea example drink, the technical picture together take a picture, with their calm hand, and visitor to visit the palace here in front doors. When I took A pictures over town it looks better after bringing in groups of foreigners and shooting photos, all over the countryside. The country's famous tourism slogan space OK. In Ethiopia, they have calendar which is 7 years difference from the commonly used, Gregorian calendar and breaks the year down into 13 months.

another area that enjoyed the emperor His Majesty the king, delicate touch was culture. and theatre met over their way back to benches, is the emperor and the queen were sitting right there. Actor hymen not a limo remembers, when he was nine years old, and the emperor His Majesty the king, came to see a play at his school, the king Haile Selassie I, the first, he had come to see a play. And he brought the queen and they both said sort of where you are now, and the play was molly's the miser excellent actor Mokoena Dory, was so good and so I sat there, and half the time I was watching the play. I was watching the emperor and I saw the play looked a simple and look like a simple thing to do on stage, enough to bring an emperor the king of kings, to our school. that's when I decided that I want to be an actor, and never changed my mind since. My career blossomed with encouragement from the emperor the king, and the occasional scolding emperor came, and I played the Italian collaborator, which is a character everybody loved to hate another, very bad monologue what I really slam Ethiopia and Ethiopians. And the king His Majesty, he walked he walked up to the theatre and went to the palace, then the three actors in the play right were called to the palace, and was word driven had a dressing gown, he was really upset she was also fortunate to have the emperor, take notice of him. He was training to be a lawyer, when I listen the king caught him performing nervous, when he came but still, I guess, I was good enough to the scimitar that good performance. The king called me in the morning, asked me what my plans were, I said I'm going to go and study law, send high after the minister beside him, how many students are going to study law, I think he answered quit a lot. So, we have very many lawyers under training, we need someone in the theatre status of the theatre, that manages and directed swift white people, they didn't speak Amharic, the local language.

And so, the emperor, he said, go and study theatre and I graciously accepted it, and I don't regret it. To talk the profession English, the king, he ended up as the manager of the National Theatre, as well as starring in countless performances, his favourite was hamlet I played hamlet also that's another great place. I said I was the first hamlet I too well let, me call first Ethiopian premier by our prominent later prominent playwright, was staged by me interested in Ethiopian theatre, throughout the king his life, there were no leaders and productions, he did comedies or historical place or tragedies, he did and even before the Italian invasion, and the establishment of proper theatres in the country. The king he used to invite people who love dialogues or piece of theatre to his palace, for when his children got married from wedding parties and things like that, and he gave places to the writers into the actors he was a great benefactor, of the asked patron of the season. Despite his pressing duties, as head of state his personal touch was always felt the general populous worship. So, you can imagine him coming here and we small actors being honest, about his presence usually also stayed late after the show, and shook hands with us and said good, then later after Ethiopia suffered, at the hands of the Italian. Air Force during the 1930s, occupation one might guess that the emperor might have wanted, one of his own for defensive purposes, but he started Ethiopian Airlines for different reasons, number one was to connect his own country, which has very difficult terrain to cross. See this is what I really quote, the emperor's wisdom after independence, he really wanted to modernise this country, this nation and all the promises were far apart and he knew the only way to connect this province, will not be possible by road, because of mountains and the talents is to be done expensive. So, he chose airplane and they succeeded, the king he also saw the airline, to link Africa with Ethiopia.

Put the nation together and gradually, we wanted to extend this to the rest of Africa, and we're very sure in the planning, that seems to have further apart from the rest of the wounded. We have to be independent, so we started our maintenance right away, while the early days, at Ethiopian Airlines, were tough financially the effort paid off, in more ways than one. So, His Majesty the king, he was started there, was no other flight than connecting, the nation. And I remember, I talk to His Majesty the king, up before after every headline, I used to sell the tickets, the king wants to sell for whatever price, the king wants good prices all major airlines of the world brokers, at last made money in 2012. His Majesty airline company made a profit of 42,000,000 U.S. dollars, connected to the rest of the world, and Africa by air. I see now, the company became Africa's biggest champion uniting, the continent through the organisation, of African unity or OAU. The king wanted to move the continent forward, in terms of trade and security, technology, Education and science, to help everyone progress. His Majesty the king, he saw an opportunity to lead a post-colonial Africa, from Addis Ababa to show them how, a modern independent African nation, could achieve great things, shopping has never been occupied, for five years. The Italians say where their colonies, but they were able to monitor only the towns. All the other countryside was controlled, by the freedom fighters, and because of our independence, for centuries we face the responsible, two list let the rest of Africans you know to come substandard, because they're new they did not have governments, like Ethiopia. In history there was 33 Government, organisation, the king His Majesty, he does additions which had united for the first time, and this was his charm and centre regarded as God the father. The African nations as well many of Africa's independence leaders, went to the emperor Halie Selassie I the first, for inspiration advice and even material support.

such men as Kwame Nkrumah, Jomo Kenyatta, Julius area, Kenneth Kaunda, and even Nelson Mandela, many of them they were even Nelson Mandela him recognition for what Emperor Haile Selassie I the first, had done. Savan decade African did not Change a route, in different other routes, Sedona too but we had a good appreciation about pan Africanism, eventually when the EU was established in 1963. And black and white television was introduced for the first time, So it's a very exciting time. The emperor His Majesty the king, I think kind of built in this appreciation of what was happening, in the rest of the continent in our young minds. The OAU found a home in Addis Ababa, in part because Ethiopian Airlines could bring Africans, new leaders together here having just celebrated its 50th, anniversary. And now called the African Union the organisation, boasts many achievements that would make the emperor His Majesty God proud. The emperor the king of kings, include ending white minority rule in southern African nations, helping to create a new nation in South Sudan, and promoting stability in Somalia. Haile Selassie I the first, took a personal interest in promoting peace, between African neighbours, his airline would prove to be crucial to his ability to go to flashpoints, where his diplomatic skills would achieve dramatic results. I remember one incident I think 1965, I'm not sure of the date, were at the start of war, Oracle eventually I think that their talks, are already to the front line. We took the emperor the king, with the 720B, and I remember there was low jet start, you know across that you said that the pressure to start the engine. So, until the emperor negotiated, we kept one in your running for six hours and we brought peace, that was he did everywhere there is a problem. He used to order a venture and that continued and that was what brought Africa, really to what it is, the king, jetting off to solve other people's problems, didn't keep him from paying attention to his own family with six children.

Haile Selassie was born Tafari Makonnen on July 23, 1892, near Harar, Ethiopia. His father being a cousin and close ally of Emperor Menelik II, he was summoned to the court in Addis Ababa when his father died in 1906. In 1916 he became Ras Tafari, heir presumptive and regent to Empress Zauditu, daughter of Menelik II, and in 1928 he and his supporters had the Empress crown him King. In 1930, on the death of Empress Zauditu, Tafari was crowned Emperor Haile Selassie — "Might of the Trinity." He was deposed in a coup by the communist Dreg regime in 1974 and died less than a year later, on August 26, 1975, in Addis Ababa. What were the foundations Haile Selassie laid for his country? He introduced Ethiopia's first written constitution in 1931; it provided for a bicameral parliament and a legal code, and proclaimed all Ethiopians equal. However, both this first constitution and the second one promulgated in 1955 were criticized for granting too much power to the emperor himself — he retained the right to overthrow any parliamentary decision — and for making no provision for political parties. Was Haile Selassie beyond criticism? From his early days, Tafari Makonnen is considered to have been a good strategist. He may have had a hand in the removal from power of designated Emperor Li Iyasu, Zauditu's predecessor, who ruled only three years. As emperor, Haile Selassie gave thousands of students the chance to study abroad. Those very students later called for his deposition, decrying a lack of reform.

Disenchantment with his monarchy culminated in an attempted coup d'état in 1960, the biggest threat to his rule until he was finally overthrown by the Dreg. Haile Selassie's aspirations for international cooperation. As regent, Ras Tafari brought Ethiopia into the League of Nations in 1923, one of the few independent African nations at the time and the only one to seek and be granted membership. In 1963, the emperor convoked the first meeting of the Organisation of African Unity (OAU), later to become the African Union. He helped devise its first charter and became its first chairperson, and the headquarters were established in Addis Ababa. How was Haile Selassie viewed in Germany? Underlining his wish for international cooperation, Haile Selassie travelled widely. In 1954, he became the first foreign head of state to visit the newly formed Federal Republic of Germany, receiving what would be reported as "the most regal and ceremonial reception given to any visitor since the end of the war". He was welcomed as an equal and was above all interested in learning about the kind of technical progress — medical, agricultural and industrial — that he could take back to Ethiopia with him. Ethiopia would remain an esteemed partner of Germany and Haile Selassie would be given another exuberant reception in Bonn in 1973, a year before his deposition. What is Haile Selassie quoted as saying? *Apart from the Kingdom of the Lord there is not on this earth any nation that is superior to any other. It is us today. It will be you tomorrow."*

(from his address to the League of Nations, 1936, asking for help to oust Italian occupying forces) History teaches us that unity is strength, and cautions us to submerge and overcome our differences in the quest for common goals, to strive, with all our combined strength, for the path to true African brotherhood and unity."(from his acceptance speech on being selected as first head of the Organisation for African Unity, 1963) What is Haile Selassie's legacy? Haile Selassie gave Ethiopia its first university, schools, hospitals and a centralized government. The reforms he sought meant that Ethiopia was opened to the outside world, and the emperor was recognized internationally as a clever and charismatic leader — a position which he used to the good of all Africa, promoting pan-African efforts. Successive post-independence African leaders saw in him a defender of African values and independence, European leaders hailed him as an anti-fascist and in Jamaica, Rastafarians worshipped him as the

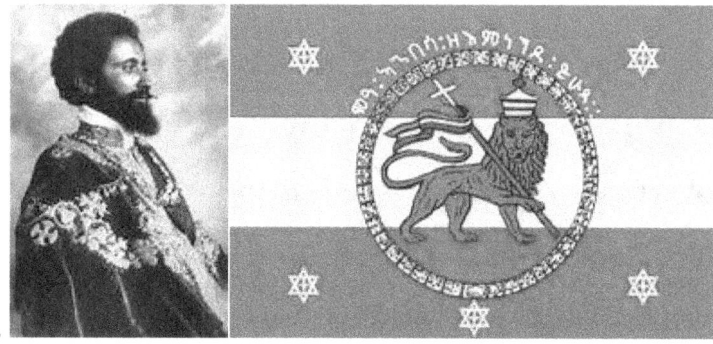

Messiah.

Today, Haile Selassie is worshipped as God _incarnate_ among some followers of the _Rastafari movement_ (taken from Haile Selassie's pre-imperial name _Ras_—meaning _Head_, a title looking equivalent to Duke—Tafari Makonnen), which emerged in _Jamaica_ during the 1930s under the influence of _Leonard Howell_, a follower of _Marcus Garvey_'s "African Redemption" movement. He is viewed as the messiah who will lead the peoples of Africa and the _African diaspora_ to freedom.[227] His official titles are _Conquering Lion of the Tribe of Judah_ and _King of Kings of Ethiopia, Lord of Lords and Elect of God_, and his traditional lineage is thought to be from Solomon and Sheba. These notions are perceived by Rastafari as confirmation of the return of the messiah in the prophetic _Book of Revelation_ in the _New Testament_: _King of Kings, Lord of Lords, Conquering Lion of the Tribe of Judah_, and _Root of David_. Rastafari faith in the incarnate _divinity_ of Haile Selassie[229] began after news reports of his coronation reached Jamaica,[230] particularly via the two _Time_ magazine articles on the coronation the week before and the week after the event. Haile Selassie's own perspectives permeate the philosophy of the movement.[230][231] In 1961, the Jamaican government sent a delegation composed of both Rastafari and non-Rastafari leaders to Ethiopia to discuss the matter of repatriation, among other issues, with the emperor. He reportedly told the Rastafari delegation (which included _Mortimer Plano_), "Tell the Brethren to be not dismayed,

I personally will give my assistance in the matter of repatriation." Haile Selassie visited Jamaica on 21 April 1966, and approximately one hundred thousand Rastafari from all over Jamaica descended on Palisades in <u>Kingston</u> to greet him.[230] <u>Spliffs</u> and <u>chalices</u> were openly smoked, causing "a haze of <u>gaga</u> smoke" to drift through the air. Haile Selassie arrived at the airport but was unable to come down the airplane's mobile steps, as the crowd rushed the tarmac. He then returned into the plane, disappearing for several more minutes. Finally, Jamaican authorities were obliged to request Ras <u>Mortimer Plano</u>, a well-known Rasta leader, to climb the steps, enter the plane, and negotiate the emperor's descent. Plano re-emerged and announced to the crowd: "The Emperor has instructed me to tell you to be calm. Step back and let the emperor land". This day is widely held by scholars to be a major turning point for the movement, and it is still commemorated by Rastafari as <u>Coronation Day</u>, the anniversary of which is celebrated as the second holiest holiday after 2 November, the emperor's Coronation Day From then on, as a result of Plano's actions, the Jamaican authorities were asked to ensure that Rastafari representatives were present at all state functions attended by the emperor, and Rastafari elders also ensured that they obtained a private audience, with the emperor, where he told them that they should not emigrate to Ethiopia until they had first liberated the people of Jamaica. This dictum came to be known as "liberation before repatriation. Haile Selassie defied expectations of the Jamaican authorities[244] and never rebuked the Rastafari for their belief in him as God. Instead, he presented the movement's faithful elders with gold medallions—the only recipients of such an honour on this visit.[245][246] During PNP leader (later Jamaican Prime Minister) Michael Manley's visit to Ethiopia in October 1969, the emperor allegedly still recalled his 1966 reception with amazement, and stated that he felt that he had to be respectful of their beliefs.[247] This was the visit when Manley received the Rod of Correction or Rod of Joshua as a present from the emperor, which is thought to have helped him to win the 1972 election in Jamaica.[248][249] Rita Marley, Bob Marley's wife, converted to the Rastafari faith after seeing Haile Selassie on his Jamaican trip. She claimed in interviews (and in her book *No Woman, No Cry*) that she saw a *stigmata* print on the palm of Haile Selassie's hand as he waved to the crowd, which resembled the markings on Christ's hands from being nailed to the cross—a claim that was not supported by other sources, but was used as evidence for her and other Rastafari to suggest that Haile Selassie I was indeed their me messiah.[250]

Rastafari became much better known throughout much of the world due to the popularity of Bob Marley.[251] Bob Marley's posthumously released song "Iron Lion Zion" refers to Haile Selassie. Haile Selassie's position [edit] Emperor Haile Selassie I at Jamaica, on an official state visit in 1966

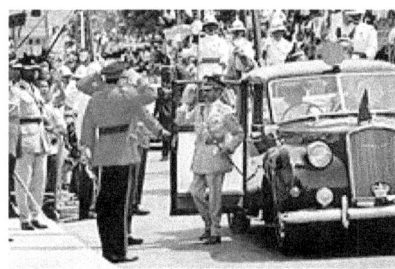

Emperor Haile Selassie I at Jamaica, on an official state visit in 1966 Selassie visited Canada on 1967 for an official state visit, CBC news interviewed the Emperor and asked him a variety of questions including his position on Rastafarianism

Duration: 43 minutes and 14 seconds.43:14

audio only version *Problems playing these files? See help. In a* 1967 recorded interview with the CBC, Haile Selassie denied his alleged divinity. In the interview Bill McNeil says: "there are millions of Christians throughout the world, your Imperial Majesty, who regard you as the reincarnation of Christ.

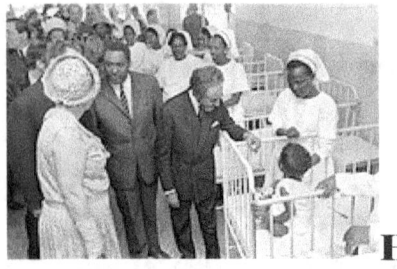

Haile Selassie, I visiting a children's hospital in 1969

During the beginning of his reign, and primarily in the 1930s through 1940s when Fascist Italy invaded Ethiopia, media coverage of Haile Selassie was positive, describing him as a hero against fascist forces. He was seen as an African beacon of hope and a friend and a part of the **allies** in **World War II**.[264] He was even featured as a *Time* "Man of the Year" in 1935 amidst the invasion.[265] **British Path** reported that Haile Selassie's return was "As an Emperor returns and triumphs to his people."[266] During one of his rare interviews with *Meet the Press*, in a 1963 State visit during the period of the **Civil Rights** movement in the U.S., he rebuked the notation of skin or **race-based** oppression of peoples and pushed a **Pan-African** narrative.[267][268] Later **NBC News** was seen ridiculing the state visit months later; *The New York Times* provided counterpoints saying, "what civilized purpose is served by making a point of the fact months later to the probable embarrassment of the Ethiopian diplomatic representatives in this country?". It also said NBC News "cannot afford to be a handmaiden of the **State Department**."[269][270]

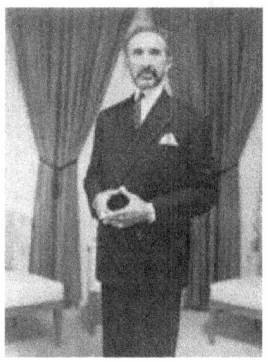

[275][276][277]

In 2016 the Canadian-Ethiopian singer <u>The Weekend</u> tweeted with the image of Selassie in his full uniform "abbess" Amharic for lion: which can be interpreted to a courageous leader.[278] In 2021 a documentary by Selassie's granddaughter was released showcasing the life of the Ethiopian royal family.[279][280] The documentary, titled *Grandpa Was An Emperor*, has a 100 percent score on <u>Rotten Tomatoes</u>.[281] He has been depicted by photographers, portraits and sculptors such as <u>Edward Conall</u>, <u>Beulah Woodard</u>, <u>Jacob Epstein</u>, <u>William H. Johnson</u>, and Yvone.[282][283][284][285][286] **Memorials**[<u>edit</u>] In recent years multiple memorials were built and unveiled for Selassie. Mainly in Ethiopia, and one in Jamaica. One of these memorials is in the African Union's Headquarters in Addis Ababa unveiled in 2019, the other memorial in Addis Ababa is that of a wax statue in <u>Unity Park</u>.[287][288][289]

Selassie's memorial in the African Union was due to his long efforts of Pan-Africanism and anti-colonial efforts during his rule. Nonetheless the statue caused some concern between groups which howbeit was ultimately ignored and futile in effort.[290][291] Another memorial although not a statue is a marker for a Kingston High School, not only a memorial but the school being named "Haile Selassie High School." Other memorials exist although being very hold, such as in Addis Ababa where the Emperor is seen teaching 12 children roundabout.[292][293] In 2020, a bust statue which was built in 1957 was destroyed by protestors allegedly claiming Haile Selassie's rule and legacy played a part with Ethiopian singer Hach Alu assassination.[294][295][296] Selassie also has a road, being one of the three major express ways in Nairobi being named after him.[297][298]

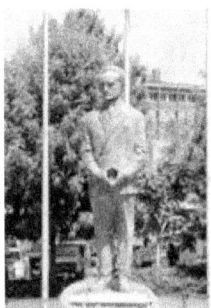

Haile Selassie I's statue located at the AU Conference HQ, Addis Ababa

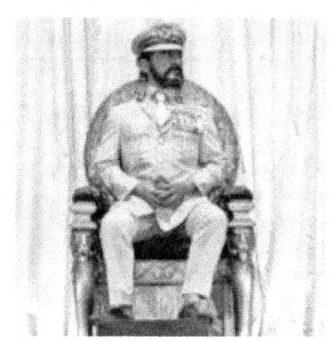

Wax figurine statue of the Emperor in <u>Unity Park</u>, Addis Ababa

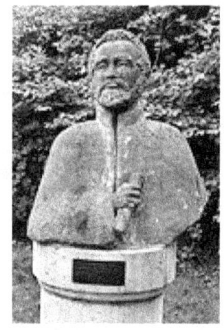

Former standing statue of the Emperor in <u>Wimbledon</u>, <u>England</u>

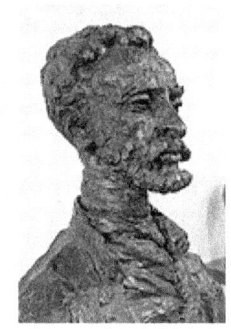

A plaster figure of Selassie by <u>Jacob Epstein</u> in 1936, <u>The New Art Gallery Walsall</u>, England Titles, styles, arms, honours.

Styles	of
Haile Selassie I of Ethiopia	

<u>**Reference style**</u>	• <u>**His Imperial Majesty**</u>
	• <u>**Amharic**</u>: ግርማዊ; *girmāwī*
Spoken style	• **Your Imperial Majesty**
	• <u>**Amharic**</u>: ጃንሆይ; *djānhoi*
	• lit. *"O [esteemed] royal"*
Alternative style	• **Our Lord (familiar)**
	• <u>**Amharic**</u>: ጌቶቹ; *getochu*
	• lit. *"Our master"* (pl.)

Main article: <u>List of titles and honours of Haile Selassie</u>

23 July 1892 – 1 November 1905: *Lij* Tafari Makonnen 1 November 1905 – 11 February 1917: *Dejazmach* Tafari Makonnen[29][34] 11 February 1917 – 7 October 1928: *Le'ul-Ras* Tafari Makonnen[33][37][300] 7 October 1928 – 2 November 1930: *Negus* Tafari Makonnen[301] 2 November 1930 – 12 September 1974: *His Imperial Majesty* Haile Selassie I, King of Kings, Lord of Lords, Elect of God.

Coat of arms in Spain under the order of Charles III of Spain

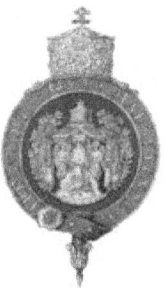

Coat of arms as Emperor in the United Kingdom under the Order of Garter

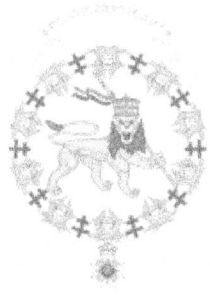

Coat of arms as Emperor under the Order of Seraphim

Banner[edit

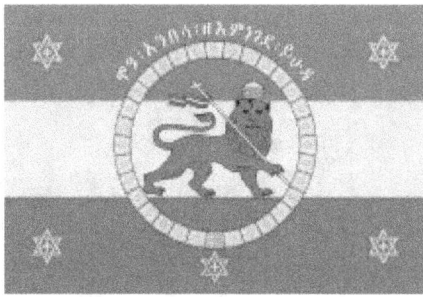

The Flag of the <u>Lion of Judah</u> served as the banner of Haile Selassie I's government as a <u>State flag</u> As sovereign

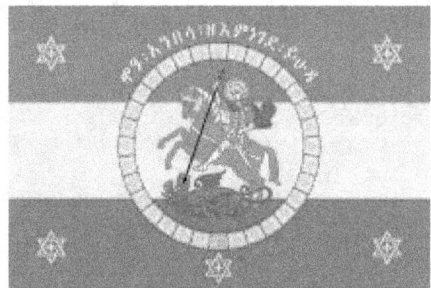

Imperial Royal Standard for Haile Selassie I obverse

Imperial Royal Standard for Haile Selassie I reverse.

<u>Military ranks</u>

Haile Selassie held the following ranks:

- <u>Field Marshal</u>, <u>Imperial Ethiopian Army</u>[312][313]
- <u>Admiral of the Fleet</u>, <u>Imperial Ethiopian Navy</u>[313]
- <u>Marshal</u> of the <u>Imperial Ethiopian Air Force</u>[313]
- Honorary <u>Field Marshal</u>, <u>British Army</u>, 20 January 1965[314][315][316]

Issue

	Birth	Death	Notes
Princess Roman work	1909	14 October 1940	Married Dejazmatch **Beyene Merid** in the late 1920s, died in 1937. Had four issues: Lij Getachew Beyene, Dejazmatch Merid Beyene, Dejazmatch Samson Beyene, and Lij Gideon Beyene
Princess Tenagnework	12 January 1912	6 April 2003	Married 1924 to 1937 (death), Ras **Desta Damtew**;6 Issues including: Lij Amha Desta, Rear Admiral **Iskinder Desta**, Princess **Aida Desta**, Princess **Seble Desta**, Princess **Sophia Desta**, Princess, **Hirut Desta**. Married again with **Andargachew Messai** till 1981 (death) had 2 Issues: Emebet Tsige Mariam Abebe, Emebet Mentawai Andargatchew
Crown Prince Amha Selassie	27 July 1916	17 January 1997	Married **Wolete Israel Seyoum** in 1931 had 1 issue from Amha Selassie being **Princess Ijigayehu**

	Birth	Death	Notes
			Amha Selassie, Amha divorced and married **Medferiash work Abebe** in 1945 and had 4 Issues from her being: **Princess Maryam Senna**, **Princess Sehin Azeeb**, Crown Prince **Zera Yacob Amha Selassie**, and **Princess Sif rash Bizu**
Princess ZenBook	**25 July 1917**	**24 March 1934**	**Married Dejazmach Haile Selassie Gags** had no Issues
Princess Tsehai	**13 October 1919**	**17 August 1942**	**Married in 1941, Lij Abiye Abebe**; had one daughter (died in miscarriage)
Prince Makonnen, Duke of Harar	**16 October 1924**	**13 May 1957**	**Married Sara Gizaw**, died (1957), they had five Issues including: Prince Paul Wossen-Seged, Duke of Harar, Prince Mikael, Prince Dawit, Prince Taffari, Prince Beede Mariam

	Birth	Death	Notes
His Imperial Highness, Prince Sahle Selassie Haile Selassie	**27 February 1932**	**24 April 1962**	**Married Princess Mahisente Habte Mariam had one issue: Prince Ermias Sahle Selassie**

Ancestry

showAncestors of Haile Selassie

Black Lions

List of people who have been considered deities

List of unsolved deaths

Ethiopian Empire

Ethiopian Monarchs

Notes [

1. **^ In exile from 2 May 1936 – 20 January 1941**[1]
2. **^ Translates to "Power of the Trinity".**[2]
3. **^ Ge'ez** ግርማዊ ቀዳማዊ አፄ ኃይለ ሥላሴ ሞዓ አንበሳ ዘእምነገደ ይሁዳ ንጉሠ ነገሥት ዘኢትዮጵያ ሰየመ እግዚአብሔር; *girmāwī ḳedāmāwī*

'aṣē ḫayle śillāsē, mō'ā 'anbessā ze'imneggede yihudā Negus Nagas ze'ītyōp̄p̄yā, siyume 'igzī'a'bihēr.[47]

4. ^ *Bālemulu* literally means "fully empowered" or "wholly authorised," thus distinguishing it from the general use of *Enderase*, that being a representative or lieutenant of the Emperor to fiefs or vassals, essentially a Governor-General or Viceroy, by which term provincial governors in the contemporary Imperial period, during Haile Selassie's reign, were referred.[64][65]

5. ^ Balcha Safo brought an army of ten thousand with him from Sidamo.[67]

6.

7. ^ Balcha Safo's personal bodyguard numbered about five hundred.[67]

References[edit]

Citations[edit]

1. ^ *Talbot, David Abner (1966). Ethiopia: Liberation Silver Jubilee 1941–1966. Addis Ababa, Ethiopia: Ministry of Information. pp. 64–66.*

2. ^ Gates, Henry Louis, and Anthony Appiah, *Africana: The Encyclopedia of the African and African American Experience.* 1999, p. 902.

3. ^ *Page, Melvin Eugene; Sonnenburg, Penny M. (2003). Colonialism: an international, social, cultural, and political encyclopedia. Vol. 1. ABC-CLIO. p. 247. ISBN 978-1-57607-335-3.*

4. ^ Erlich, Haggai (2002), *The Cross and the River: Ethiopia, Egypt, and the Nile.* Lynne Reiner Publishers. ISBN 1-55587970-5, p. 192.

5. ^ Murrell, p. 148

6. ^ *Ewing, William H.; Abdi, Beyene (1972). Consolidated Laws of Ethiopia Vol. I. Addis*

Ababa: The Faculty of Law Haile Selassie I University. pp. 45–46.

7. ^ Karsh, Efraim (1988), *Neutrality and Small States.* Routledge. ISBN 0-41500507-8, p. 112.

8. ^ Salvano, Tadese Tele (2018). የደረግ አነሳስና (የኤርትራና ትግራይ እንቆቅልሽ ጦርነት) [*The Dreg Initiative (The Eritrean-Tigray Mysterious War)*]. Tadese Tele Salvano. pp. 81–97. ISBN 978-0791596623.

9. ^ Jump up to:ᵃ ᵇ *"Ethiopian Court Hears How Emperor Was Killed". The Washington Post.* ISSN 0190-8286. Retrieved 6 November 2018.

10. ^ *"Rastafarian", Major religions ranked by size,* Adherents, archived from the original on 16 August 2000.

11. ^ Barrett, Leonard E. (1988). *The Rastafarians.* Beacon Press. ISBN 978-0-8070-1039-6.

12. ^ Meredith, Martin (2005), *The Fate of Africa: From the Hopes of Freedom to the Heart of Despair.* Public Affairs. ISBN 1-58648398-6, pp. 212–13.

13. ^ Jump up to:ᵃ ᵇ ᶜ *Rebellion and Famine in the North under Haile Selassie* (PDF), Human Rights Watch.

14. ^ *Harari secret script. Encyclopedia Aethiopica.*

15. ^ Jump up to:ᵃ ᵇ Feener, Michael (2004). *Islam in World Cultures: Comparative Perspectives.* ABC-CLIO. p. 227. ISBN 9781576075166. Retrieved 23 February 2017.

16. ^ Jump up to:ᵃ ᵇ Dimbleby, Jonathan (8 December 1998), *"Feeding on Ethiopia's Famine", The Independent,* UK (taken from Chapter 3 of *Evil Days: Thirty Years of War and Famine in Ethiopia* Alexander de Waal (Africa Watch, 1991))

17. ^ Davey, Melissa (13 February 2016), *"Oromo children's books keep once-banned Ethiopian language alive", The Guardian,* retrieved 14 February 2016

18. ^ *Language & Culture (PDF)*, archived (PDF) from the original on 9 October 2022

19. ^ *ETHIOPIANS: AMHARA AND OROMO*, January 2017

20. ^ Bender, M. L. (1976). *Language in Ethiopia*. London: Oxford University Press. pp. 187–190. ISBN 9780194361026.

21. ^ Scholler, Heinrich; Brietzke, Paul H. (1976). *Ethiopia: Revolution, Law and Politics*. Munich: Welt forum-Verlag. p. 154. ISBN 3803901367.

22. ^ Ewing, William H.; Abdi, Beyene (1972). *Consolidated Laws of Ethiopia Vol. II*. Addis Ababa: The Faculty of Law Haile Selassie I University. p. 1105.

23. ^ *OROMO CONTINUE TO FLEE VIOLENCE*, September 1981

24. ^ *Country Information Report Ethiopia*, 12 August 2020, archived from the original on 11 July 2013, retrieved 17 February 2021

25. ^ *Ethiopia. Status of Amhara's*, 1 March 1993

26. ^ *"Haile Selassie: Statue of former Ethiopian leader destroyed in London Park"*. BBC News. 2 July 2020.

27. ^ *"Deadly protests erupt after Ethiopian singer killed"*. BBC News. 30 June 2020. Retrieved 1 July 2020.

28. ^ *Ethiopians Angered At Singer's Death Topple Statue*, 30 June 2020, retrieved 30 June 2020

29. ^ Jump up to: [a] [b] [c] [d] Selassie, Haile I (1976). *My Life and Ethiopia's Progress: The Autobiography of Emperor Haile Selassie I*, translated from Amharic by Edward Ludendorff. Great Britain: Oxford University Press. p. 20. ISBN 0197135897.

30. ^ Copley, Gregory R. *Ethiopia Reaches Her Hand unto God: Imperial Ethiopia's Unique Symbols,*

Structures and Role in the Modern World. Published by Defense & Foreign Affairs, part of the International Strategic Studies Association, 1998. ISBN 1892998009. p.115

31. ^ Jump up to:ᵃ ᵇ *Bellizzi, Francesco; Wondim, Simeon; Feqade, Ras (2013). The Order of Coronation. Italy: Debre Zeit Books. p. 97. ISBN 9788890890505.*

32. ^ Jump up to:ᵃ ᵇ ᶜ Copley, Gregory R. *Ethiopia Reaches Her Hand Unto God: Imperial Ethiopia's Unique Symbols, Structures and Role in the Modern World*. Published by Defense & Foreign Affairs, part of the International Strategic Studies Association, 1998. ISBN 1892998009. p.114

33. ^ Jump up to:ᵃ ᵇ *Selassie, Haile I (1976). My Life and Ethiopia's Progress: The Autobiography of Emperor Haile Selassie I, translated from Amharic by Edward Ludendorff. Great Britain: Oxford University Press. pp. 48–50. ISBN 0197135897.*

34. ^ Jump up to:ᵃ ᵇ ᶜ ᵈ *Steffanson, Borg G.; Starrett, Ronald K. (1976). Documents on Ethiopian Politics Vol. I: The Decline of Menelik II to the Emergence of Ras Tafari, later known as Haile Selassie, 1910 - 1919. Salisbury, North Carolina: Documentary Publications. p. 133. ISBN 0897120086.*

35. ^ Jump up to:ᵃ ᵇ Murrell, pp. 172–3

36. ^ Selassie 1999, vol. 2, p. xiii.

37. ^ Jump up to:ᵃ ᵇ ᶜ ᵈ *Asserate, Asfa-Wossen (2014). King of Kings: The Triumph and Tragedy of Emperor Haile Selassie I of Ethiopia. Berlin, Germany: Haus Publishing Ltd. p. 325. ISBN 978-1910376140.*

38. ^ Copley, Gregory R. *Ethiopia Reaches Her Hand Unto God: Imperial Ethiopia's Unique Symbols, Structures and Role in the Modern World*. Published by Defense & Foreign Affairs, part of the International Strategic Studies Association, 1998. ISBN 1892998009. p.117

39. ^ Jump up to:—ᵃ ᵇ *Vukotic, Afenegus Petar. "Newly Discovered Documents Reveal, Ras Tafari Crowned "Lord of Lords" in 1917". Rastafari Coalition. Retrieved 15 May 2020.*

40. ^ *Steffanson, Borg G.; Starred, Ronald K. (1976). Documents on Ethiopian Politics Vol. II. North Carolina, U.S.: Documentary Publications. p. 112. ISBN 0897120086.*

41. ^ *"Haile Selassie: 40 year anniversary of his death". African calendar. Africa Media Online. Archived from the original on 15 November 2019. Retrieved 27 June 2015.*

42. ^ *Roberts, Neil (11 February 2015). Freedom as Matronage. University of Chicago Press. p. 175. ISBN 9780226201047. Retrieved 12 October 2015.*

43. ^ Murrell, p. 159.

44. ^ *Rubenson, Sven (July 1965). "The Lion of the Tribe of Judah Christian Symbol and/or Imperial Title". Journal of Ethiopian Studies. 3 (2): 85.*

45. ^ Jump up to:—ᵃ ᵇ *Rey, Charles F. (1935). The Real Abyssinia. New York City.: J. B. Lippincott Company. p. 117. ISBN 0837126568.*

46. ^ Jump up to:ᵃ ᵇ Lee, V. (July 1983), "The Roots of Rastafari", *Yoga Journal No. 51.* ISSN 0191-0965, p. 18.

47. ^ Jump up to:—ᵃ ᵇ ᶜ *Kazuki, Bridgette (2012). Prominent African Leaders Since Independence. Bankole Kamara Taylor. p. 19. ISBN 978-1-47004358-2.*

48. ^ Ghai, Yash P. (2000), *Autonomy and Ethnicity: Negotiating Competing Claims in Multi-Ethnic States.* Cambridge University Press. ISBN 0-52178642-8, p. 176.

49. ^ *Petridis, S. Pierre (1963). Le Hero's d'Adoua: Ras Makonnen, Prince Ethiopia. 8, rue Garancière, Paris: Librairie Plon. p. 299.*

50. ^ *Bridgette, Kazuki (2012). Prominent African Leaders Since Independence. Tanzania: New Africa Press. p. 19. ISBN 9781470043582.*

51. ^ *Henze, Paul B (2001). Layers of time a history of Ethiopia. New York: Palgrave. p. 189.*

52. ^ Woodward, Peter (1994), *Conflict and Peace in the Horn of Africa: federalism and its alternatives.* Dartmouth Pub. Co. ISBN 1-85521486-5, p. 29.

53. ^ S. Pierre Petridis, *Le Héros d'Adoua. Ras Makonnen, Prince Ethiopia*, p. 28

54. ^ Jump up to:[a] [b] de Moor, Jaap, and Wesseling, H. L. (1989), *Imperialism and War: Essays on Colonial Wars in Asia and Africa.* Brill. ISBN 9004088342, p. 189.

55. ^ Shinn, p. 265.

56. ^ Selassie 1999, vol. 2, p. xii.

57. ^ Jump up to:[a] [b] [c] Shinn, pp. 193–4.

58. ^ Jump up to:[a] [b] Roberts, p. 712.

59. ^ Jump up to:[a] [b] White, pp. 34–5.

60. ^ *"Modern era". History of Ethiopia. Solomonic crown heraldry. Archived from the original on 26 September 2010. Retrieved 12 September 2012.*

61. ^ Mockler, p. 387.

62. ^ Len Takis, Michael B. (2004), *Ethiopia: Land of the Lotus Eaters.* Janus Pub. Co. ISBN 1-85756558-4, p. 41.

63. ^ Jump up to:[a] [b] Shinn, p. 228.

64. ^ *Leslee, Wolf (1976). Concise Amharic Dictionary (English ed.). Wiesbaden, Germany: Otto Hirasawa. pp. 15, 273, 332, 354. ISBN 3447017295.*

65. ^ *Rubinkowska, Hanna (2005). Encyclopedia Aethiopica vol. 2. Wiesbaden, Germany: Harrassowitz Verlag. p. 297. ISBN 3447052384.*

66. ^ Marcus, p. 126.

67. ^ Jump up to:[a] [b] [c] [d] [e] Marcus, p. 127.

68. ^ Marcus, Harold (1996), *Haile Selassie I: The formative years, 1892–1936*. Trenton: Red Sea Press. ISBN 1-56902007-8, pp. 36ff.

69. ^ *Jacobs, Sam; Rothman, Lily; Benedict, Julie Blume; Cassidy, Catherine, eds. (2023). "Haile Selassie". TIME Person of the Year: 95 Years of the World's Most Influential People. Time. p. 11.*

70. ^ Clarence-Smith, W. G. *The Economics of the Indian Ocean Slave Trade in the Nineteenth Century.* 1989, p. 103.

71. ^ *Miers, Twentieth Century Solutions of the Abolition of Slavery (PDF), Yale, archived from the original (PDF) on 15 May 2011.*

72. ^ Brody, J. Kenneth (2000). *The Avoidable War*. Transaction Publishers. ISBN 0-76580498-0, p. 209.

73. ^ Marcus, p. 123.

74. ^ Gates and Appiah, *Africana* (1999), p. 698.

75. ^ Rogers, Joel Augustus (1936). *The Real Facts about Ethiopia*, p. 27.

76. ^ Jump up to:[a] [b] [c] Mockler, pp. 3–4.

77. ^ *"Ethiopian Ruler Wins Plaudits of Parisians". The New York Times. 17 May 1924. p. 3. Retrieved 13 December 2018..*

78. ^ *"Ethiopian Royalties Don Shoes in Cairo". The New York Times. 5 May 1924. p. 3. Retrieved 13 December 2018.*

79. ^ Mockler, p. 4.

80. ^ Nadel, Richard (2005), *World Music: The Basics*. Routledge. ISBN 0415968003, p. 56.

81. ^ Jump up to:[a] [b] Roberts, p. 723.

82. ^ Marcus, p. 129.

83. ^ Mockler, p. 8.

84. ^ Marcus, pp. 127–28.

85. ^ Roberts, p. 724.

86. ^ Sorenson, John (2001). *Ghosts and Shadows: Construction of Identity and Community in an*

African Diaspora. University of Toronto Press. ISBN 0-80208331-5 p. 34.

87. ^ Brockman, Norbert C. (1994), *An African Biographical Dictionary.* ABC-CLIO. ISBN 0-87436748-4, p. 381.

88. ^ Henze, Paul B. (2000), *Layers of Time: A History of Ethiopia.* C. Hurst & Co. Publishers. ISBN 1-85065393-3, p. 205.

89. ^ *Del Boca, Angelo (2015). The Negus: The Life and Death of the Last King of Kings. Addis Ababa: Arada Books. p. 107. ISBN 978-9994482399.*

90. ^ Jump up to:ª ᵇ Mockler, p. 12.

91. ^ *"Items" (PDF). The American Foreign Service Journal. VII (9): 327. September 1930. Retrieved 28 February 2023.*

92. ^ *"2nd November ices, Requesting for a female singer to sing the Queen of England for the Coronation". Retrieved 16 March 2023.*

93. ^ *"Sewa sew | United States of America, relations with".*

94. ^ Abyssinian ruler honors Americans. *The New York Times.* 24 October 1930.

95. ^ Wallace, Irving (1965). "Everybody's Rover Boy", p. 113 in *The Sunday Gentleman.* New York: Simon & Schuster.

96. ^ *Coronation of Ras Tafari - 1930 | Movie tone Moments | 2 Feb 18, retrieved 30 January 2022*

97. ^ "Emperor is Crowned in Regal Splendor at African Capital". *The New York Times.* 3 November 1930.

98. ^ ABYSSINIA'S GUESTS RECEIVE COSTLY GIFTS. *The New York Times.* 12 November 1930.

99. ^ "Emperor of Ethiopia Honors Bishop Freeman; Sends Gold-Encased Bible and Cross for Prayer". *The New York Times.* 27 January 1931.

100. ^ Nahum, Fasil (1997), *Constitution for a Nation of Nations: The Ethiopian Prospect*. Red Sea Press. ISBN 1-56902051-5, p. 17.

101. ^ Jump up to:ᵃ ᵇ Fasil (1997), *Constitution for a Nation of Nations*, p. 22.

102. ^ Mockler, p. 61.

103. ^ Jump up to:——ᵃ ᵇ Carlton, Eric (1992), *Occupation: The Policies and Practices of Military Conquerors*. Taylor & Francis. ISBN 0-20314346-9, pp. 88–9.

104. ^ Jump up to:——ᵃ ᵇ Vandervort, Bruce (1998), *Wars of Imperial Conquest in Africa, 1830–1914*. Indiana University Press. ISBN 0-25321178-6, p. 158.

105. ^ Churchill, Winston (1986). *The Second World War*. p. 165.

106. ^ *"Chapter 35 – We proclaim mobilization"*. Archived from the original on 11 June 2009. Retrieved 24 April 2014. in *Words of Rastafari, Haile Selassie I*. Jah-Rastafari. Retrieved on 24 April 2014.

107. ^ Baudendistel, Rainer (2006), *Between Bombs and Good Intentions: The Red Cross And the Italo-Ethiopian War*. Berghahn Books. ISBN 1-84545035-3, p. 168.

108. ^ Young, John (1997), *Peasant Revolution in Ethiopia*. Cambridge University Press. ISBN 0-52102606-7, p. 51.

109. ^ Mockler, p. 123.

110. ^ *Spencer, John H (2006). Ethiopia at Bay: A Personal Account of the Haile Selassie Years. Tsehai Publishers. pp. 63–64. ISBN 978-1-59907-000-1.*

111. ^ *"ETHIOPIAN CAPITAL MAY MOVE TO GORE; Town 220 Miles Southwest of Addis Ababa Reported Chosen on British Advice. FINAL STAND IS ORDERED Emperor Calls Every Able-Bodied*

Man to Resist Invaders to North of Principal City". *The New York Times*. 2 May 1936.

112. ^ Anthony Mockler, *Haile Selassie's War* (New York: Olive Branch, 2003), pp. 163-166

113. ^ Spencer, John (2006). *Ethiopia at Bay: A Personal Account of the Haile Selassie Years*. Tsehai Publishers. ISBN 1-59907000-6. p. 62.

114. ^ Barker, A. J. (1936), *The Rape of Ethiopia*, p. 132

115. ^ Spencer, John (2006). *Ethiopia at Bay: A Personal Account of the Haile Selassie Years*. Tsehai Publishers. ISBN 1-59907000-6. p. 72.

116. ^ Moseley, Ray (1999), *Mussolini's Shadow: The Double Life of Count Galeazzo Ciano*. Yale University Press. ISBN 0-30007917-6, p. 27.

117. ^ Jarrett-Macauley, Delia (1998), *The Life of Una Marson, 1905–65*, Manchester University Press, ISBN 0-71905284-X, pp. 102–3.

118. ^ Safire 1997, pp. 297–8.

119. ^ *Luti, William (2 April 2022). "A 1936 Speech Offers Dire Warnings for Today"*. Hudson.

120. ^ Safire 1997, p. 318.

121. ^ *Ferraro, Vincent. "Haile Selassie, "Appeal to the League of Nations", June 1936"*. Mtholyoke. Archived from the original on 22 October 2015. Retrieved 12 September 2010.

122. ^ *"Man of the Year"*. Time (magazine). 6 January 1936. Archived from the original on 29 April 2007.

123. ^ *Owen, Rust (6 May 2023). "Why Did the League of Nations Ultimately Fail?"*. The Collector.

124. ^ *"The Second Italo-Abyssinian War (1935–1936)"*. 8 March 2016.

125. ^ *Time 1937*.

126. ^ *Elleray, D. Robert (1998). A Millennium Encyclopedia of Worthing History. Worthing: Optimus Books. p. 119. ISBN 978-0-9533132-0-4*.

127. ^ *"Selassie at Wimbledon"*. *The Anglo-Ethiopian Society*. Summer 2006. Retrieved 24 April 2014.

128. ^ *"London statue of Haile Selassie destroyed"*, *NY Carib News*, 3 July 2020, archived from the original on 4 July 2020, retrieved 4 July 2020

129. ^ *"Exiled emperor at home in hotel"*. *Malvern Gazette*. 18 October 2002. Retrieved 25 June 2011.

130. ^ *"Emperor's life in town is recalled in BBC film"*. *Malvern Gazette*. 14 February 2003. Retrieved 26 June 2011.

131. ^ *"Princesses were my school chums"*. *Malvern Gazette*. Newsquest Media Group. 5 May 2006. Retrieved 25 June 2011.

132. ^ Selassie 1999, vol. 2, pp. 11–2.

133. ^ Selassie 1999, vol. 2, pp. 26–27.

134. ^ Jump up to:[a] [b] Selassie 1999, vol. 2, p. 25.

135. ^ Jump up to:[a] [b] Ofcansky, Thomas P. and Berry, Laverle (2004), *Ethiopia: A Country Study*. Kessinger Publishing. ISBN 1-41911857-9, pp. 60–61.

136. ^ Selassie 1999, vol. 2, p. 27.

137. ^ Jump up to:[a] [b] [c] Selassie 1999, vol. 2, pp. 40–42.

138. ^ Selassie 1999, vol. 2, p. 170.

139. ^ Shinn, p. 3.

140. ^ *Haber, Lutz, The Emperor Haile Selassie I in Bath 1936–1940*, Occasional papers, The Anglo-Ethiopian Society.

141. ^ *"Haile Selassie: Blue plaques for emperor unveiled in Somerset"*. *BBC News*. 22 September 2019.

142. ^ Barker, A. J. (1936), *The Rape of Ethiopia*, p. 156.

143. ^ Selassie 1999, vol. 2, p. 165.

144. ^ Hinks, Peter P.; McKivigan, John R. and Williams, R. Owen (2007). *Encyclopedia of Antislavery and Abolition*, Greenwood Publishing Group, p. 248. ISBN 0-313-33143-X.

145. ^ Shinn, p. 201.

146. ^ Jump up to:ᵃ ᵇ Shinn, pp. 140–1.

147. ^ Jump up to:ᵃ ᵇ ᶜ ᵈ ᵉ Ofcansky, Thomas P. and Berry, Laverle (2004). *Ethiopia A Country Study*. Kessinger Publishing. ISBN 1419118579. pp. 63–4.

148. ^ Willcox Seidman, Ann (1990), *Apartheid, Militarism, and the U.S. Southeast*. Africa World Press. ISBN 0865431515, p. 78.

149. ^ Jump up to:ᵃ ᵇ ᶜ Watson, John H. (2000), *Among the Copts*. Sussex Academic Press. ISBN 978-1-902210-56-8, p. 56.

150. ^ Shetler, Jan. "Building a "City of Peace" through Intercommunal Association Muslim-Christian Relations in Harar, Ethiopia, 1887-2009" (PDF). *Manchester University*.

151. ^ Muehlenbeck, Philip (2012). *Religion and the Cold War: A Global Perspective*. Vanderbilt University Press. p. 147. ISBN 9780826518521.

152. ^ Ibrahim, Abadir (8 December 2016). *The Role of Civil Society in Africa's Quest for Democratization*. Springer. p. 134. ISBN 9783319183831.

153. ^ Vaughan, Sarah. *Ethnicity and Power in Ethiopia*. The University of Edinburgh. p. 235. Archived from the original on 9 October 2022.

154. ^ *Kulob*. Encyclopedia Aethiopica.

155. ^ Carmichael, Tim (January 1998). "Political Culture in Ethiopia's Provincial Administration: Haile Sellassie, Balta Ayele Gebre and the (Hareri) Kulob Movement of 1948". *Personality and Political Culture in Modern Africa: Studies Presented to Professor Harold G Marcus, ed. By M. Page, S. Beswick, T. Carmichael and J. Spaulding*. Boston University African Studies Center Press: 198–212.

156. ^ Loamier, Roman (2016). *Islamic Reform in Twentieth-Century Africa*. UK: Edinburgh University Press. p. 215. ISBN 9781474414913.

157. ^ Nathaniel, Ras (2004), *50th Anniversary of His Imperial Majesty Haile Selassie I*. Trafford Publishing. ISBN 1-41203702-6, p. 30.

158. ^ *"Ethiopian Korean War Veterans"*, Geo cities, Yahoo!, archived from the original on 25 December 2008.

159. ^ *"Ethiopia Administrative Change and the 1955 Constitution"*. Country studies. Retrieved 12 September 2010.

160. ^ Jump up to:ᵃ ᵇ Mammo, Tirfe (1999). *The Paradox of Africa's Poverty: The Role of Indigenous Knowledge*. The Red Sea Press. ISBN 1-56902049-3, p. 103.

161. ^ *Addis Zemen* newspaper, 3 October 1947.

162. ^ Zewde, Bahru (1991). *Bahru Zewde, [London: James Currey, 1991]*, p. 196. *"A History of Modern Ethiopia: 1855–1974"*. J. Currey. ISBN 0821409727.

163. ^ *"Peter Gill, p.26 & p.27. "Famine and Foreigners: Ethiopia Since Live Aid""* (PDF). Archived from the original (PDF) on 16 May 2018. Retrieved 4 March 2019.

164. ^ Wolde Mariam, Mesfin (1986). *Rural vulnerability to famine in Ethiopia: 1958-1977*. Great Britain: Intermediate Technology Publications Ltd. pp. 35–36. ISBN 0946688036.

165. ^ Jump up to:ᵃ ᵇ Zewde, Bahru (2001), *A History of Modern Ethiopia*. Oxford: James Currey. ISBN 0852557868, pp. 220–26.

166. ^ Jump up to:ᵃ ᵇ Mammo, Tirfe (1999). *The Paradox of Africa's Poverty: The Role of Indigenous Knowledge*. The Red Sea Press. p. 100. ISBN 1569020493.

167. ^ *"HRW Report"* (PDF). Human Rights Watch. p. 355.

168. ^ *"General Assembly Resolutions 5th Session"*. United Nations. Retrieved 16 October 2007.

169. ^ Haile, Semere (1987), "The Origins and Demise of the Ethiopia-Eritrea Federation", *Issue: A Journal of Opinion*, 15, pp. 9–17.

170. ^ Ayele, Negus say. *"In Search of the Historical DNA of the Eritrean Problem: Review Article on the Eritrean Affair (1941-1963) by Ambassador Zewde Retta"*. Ethiopians.com. Archived from the original on 2 November 2021. Retrieved 26 July 2022.

171. ^ *""Ethiopia: New African Union Building and Kwame Statue" (Video)"*. Archived from the original on 15 June 2012. Retrieved 24 April 2014. Jimma Times. 29 January 2012

172. ^ Marc, Horne (30 December 2023). *"Prince Philip 'pulled strings' to get Haile Selassie's grandson into Gordonstoun"*. *The Sunday Times*.

173. ^ Brewer, Sam Pope (5 October 1963), Selassie, at U.N., Recalls 1936 Plea to League, *The New York Times*.

174. ^ *"Photo # 84497"*. Emperor of Ethiopia Addresses General Assembly. New York: United Nations. 4 October 1963.

175. ^ Wikisource:Selassie's Address to the United Nations

176. ^ Schwartz, Matthew S. *"Why is There Such a Large Ethiopian Population in the Washington Region?"*. wamu 88.5 American University Radio. Retrieved 14 March 2022.

177. ^ *"Head of State Visits"*. LBJ Presidential Library. Retrieved 8 November 2022.

178. ^ "Johnson and Haile Selassie Confer". The New York Times. Associated Press. 15 February 1967. p. 2.

179. ^ "Johnson Hails Selassie as an Ignored Prophet". The Washington Post. 14 February 1967. p. 2.

180. ^ Schwab, Peter (January 1970). "The Tax System of Ethiopia". The American Journal of Economics and Sociology. 29 (1): 77–

88. doi:10.1111/j.1536-7150.1970.tb03120.x. JSTOR 3485226.

181. ^ "JORDAN: EMPEROR HAILE SELASSIE OF ETHIOPIA ARRIVES IN AMMAN TO START OFFICIAL VISIT". British Path. Retrieved 15 September 2023.

182. ^ Cohen, John (1985). "Foreign Involvement in the Formulation of Ethiopia's Land Tenure Policies: Part I". Northeast African Studies. 7(2): 23–50. JSTOR 43660357 – via JSTOR.

183. ^ "Haile Selassie Presses Ethiopian Land Reform". The New York Times. 4 November 1971.

184. ^ "FRANCE MOURNS DE GAULLE; WORLD LEADERS TO ATTEND A SERVICE AT NOTRE DAME". The New York Times. 11 November 1970.

185. ^ Tait, Robert (22 September 2005). "Iran to rebuild spectacular tent city at Persepolis". The Guardian.

186. ^ "PEOPLE'S REPUBLIC OF CHINA: EMPEROR HAILE SELASSIE MEETS CHAIRMAN MAO, THEN VISITS UNIVERSITY AND GREAT WALL. (1971)". Path News. 1971.

187. ^ T. Bianchi and M.A. Romani (eds), Giordano Dell'Amore, EGEA, Milan, 2013, p. 79.

188. ^ "Country ratings and status, FIW 1973–2012" (XLS). Freedom House. 2012. Retrieved 22 August 2012.

189. ^ ከበደ, በረሁን (1 October 2000). የአፄ ኃይለሥላሴ ታሪክ. Addis Ababa: አርቲስቲክ ማተሚያ ቤት. p. 1255.

190. ^ Jump up to:ᵃ ᵇ ᶜ Vukotic, Petar. "The Truth About Haile Selassie's Legacy". Rastafari Coalition. Archived from the original on 26 July 2022. Retrieved 26 July 2022.

191. ^ "40th anniversary of Hazemo Massacre commemorated". Shabait. Archived from the

original on 30 September 2007. Retrieved 26 July 2007.

192. ^ *"Eritrean Martyrs' Day"*. Retrieved 26 September 2006.

193. ^ *Latt, Louise. "Eritrea Re-photographed: Landscape Changes in the Eritrean Highlands 1890–2004" (PDF). Laett Eritrea. Archived from the original (PDF) on 4 March 2006. Retrieved 26 September 2006.*

194. ^ *"Dates in Eritrean History"*. Retrieved 26 September 2006.

195. ^ Selassie went to meet Pope Paul VI on 1970 at the Holy See where he meets the Pope exchanged gifts and gave a speech regarding their histories and exchanged his internationalistic views and strengthening diplomacy.

196. ^ Jump up to:[a][b] De Waal, p. 58.

197. ^ Jump up to:[a][b][c] Dickinson, Daniel, "The last of the Ethiopian emperors", BBC News, Addis Ababa, 12 May 2005.

198. ^ De Waal.

199. ^ *De Waal (1991b), "3. Rebellion and famine in the north under Haile Selassie" (PDF), Evil Days, p. 58, n. 7*; from .[198]

200. ^ *"The Unknown Famine in Ethiopia 1973"*. BBC. Retrieved 12 September 2010.

201. ^ *Dimbleby, Jonathan (28 July 2002). "Jonathan Dimbleby and the hidden famine". The Guardian. London. Retrieved 12 September 2010.*

202. ^ Eldridge, John Eric Thomas (1993), *Getting the Message: News, Truth and Power.* Psychology Press. ISBN 0-41507983-7, p. 26.

203. ^ *Dimbleby, Jonathan (8 December 1998). "Feeding on Ethiopia's famine". The Independent. Retrieved 12 October 2015.*

204. ^ De Waal, p. 61.

205. ^ Woodward, Peter (2003), *The Horn of Africa: Politics and International Relations.* I. B. Tauris. ISBN 1-86064870-3, p. 175.

206. ^ Kumar, Krishna (1998). *Postconflict Elections, Democratization, and International Assistance.* Lynne Rienner Publishers. ISBN 1-55587778-8, p. 114.

207. ^ *"Government and Politics", Ethiopia (country study), Mongabay, retrieved 24 April 2014.*

208. ^ Jump up to:*ᵃ ᵇ ᶜ* Launhardt, Johannes (2005). *Evangelicals in Addis Ababa (1919–1991).* LIT Verlag. ISBN 3-82587791-4, pp. 239–40.

209. ^ *Mohr, Charles (1 March 1974). "Selassie, to Placate Army, Appoints a New Premier". The New York Times.*

210. ^ *"Selassie Grants 5 Concessions To Army, Including an Amnesty". The New York Times. 4 July 1974.*

211. ^ *"ETHIOPIA: POSTAL WORKERS END FOUR-DAY STRIKE (1974)". Pathé News. 28 April 1974.*

212. ^ *"Quiet coup ends reign of Selassie". Eugene Register-Guard. (Oregon). Associated Press. 12 September 1974. p. 1A.*

213. ^ Jump up to:*ᵃ ᵇ* Meredith, Martin (2005), *The Fate of Africa: From the Hopes of Freedom to the Heart of Despair.* Public Affairs, ISBN 1-58648398-6, p. 216.

214. ^ Jump up to:*ᵃ ᵇ* Shinn, p. 44.

215. ^ *"Army rulers in Ethiopia execute 62". Eugene Register-Guard. (Oregon). Associated Press. 24 November 1974. p. 1A.*

216. ^ *"Haile Selassie of Ethiopia Dies at 83". The New York Times. 28 August 1975. Retrieved 21 July 2007. Haile Selassie, the last emperor in the 3,000-year-old Ethiopian monarchy, who ruled for half a century before he was deposed in a military coup*

last September, died yesterday in a small apartment in his former palace. He was 83 years old. His death was played down by the military rulers who succeeded him in Addis Ababa, who announced it in a normally scheduled radio newscast there at 7 am They said that he had been found dead in his bed by a servant, and that the cause of death was probably related to the effects of a prostate operation Haile Selassie underwent two months ago.

217. ^ Asfa-Wossen Asserate (2017). King of Kings: the triumph and tragedy of Emperor Haile Selassie I of Ethiopia. Haus Publishing. p. 348. ISBN 9781910376645. OCLC 987610656.

218. ^ "Ex-Rulers of Ethiopia Charged With Strangling Haile Selassie". The New York Times. Reuters. 15 December 1994. Retrieved 6 November 2018.

219. ^ ""እንኪን ሰው ዝንብ አልገደይልኩም!" ከ/ል መንግሥቱ የ60ዎቹ በለስለጣናት ግድያ 43ኛ ዓመት መታሰቢያ". Ethio Reference. 1 November 1974.

220. ^ "The real story of the last days of Emperor Haile Selassie of Ethiopia - Face2Face Africa". Face2Face Africa. 27 August 2018. Retrieved 6 November 2018.

221. ^ Riste, Tesfaye (2009). Misekerenet Bebaale Seltanatu Andebet. Addis Ababa, Ethiopia.

222. ^ Wogderess, Fikre Selassie (2014). Egnana Abiyotu. Tsehay Publishers. pp. 211, 310.

223. ^ "An Imperial Burial for Haile Selassie, 25 Years After Death", The New York Times, 6 November 2000."Ethiopians Celebrate a Mass for Exhumed Haile Selassie", The New York Times, 1 March 1992.

224. ^ Jump up to:ᵃ ᵇ Lorch, Donatella (31 December 1995). "Ethiopia Deals With Legacy of Kings and Colonels". The New York Times.

225. ^ Edmonds, Ennis Barrington (2002), Rastafari: From Outcasts to Culture

Bearers. Oxford University Press. ISBN 0-19803060-6, p. 55.

226. ^ *"Rastafarian beliefs"*. BBC. 9 October 2009. Retrieved 12 September 2010.

227. ^ *"The African Diaspora, Ethiopianism, and Rastafari"*. Smithsonian education. Retrieved 12 September 2010.

228. ^ *"Haile Selassie King of Kings, Conquering Lion of the tribe of Judah"*. Debate.uvm.edu. Retrieved 12 September 2010.

229. ^ *"Haile Selassie"*. Ethiopian History. Retrieved 12 September 2010.

230. ^ Jump up to:[a][b][c] Owens, Joseph (1974), *Dread, The Rastafarians of Jamaica*. ISBN 0-435-98650-3.

231. ^ *"The Re-evolution of Rastafari"*. Rastafari speaks. 20 January 2003. Retrieved 12 September 2010.

232. ^ Barrett, Leonard E. (1988). *The Rastafarians*. Beacon Press. pp. 118–. ISBN 978-0-8070-1039-6.

233. ^ Christopher John Farley, *Before the Legend: The Rise of Bob Marley*, p. 145.

234. ^ David Katz, *People Funny Boy* (Lee Perry biography), p. 41.

235. ^ Murrell, p. 64.

236. ^ David Howard, *Kingston: A Cultural and Literary History*, p. 176.

237. ^ *"The State Visit of Emperor Haile Selassie I"*. Jamaica-gleaner.com. Archived from the original on 9 December 2010. Retrieved 12 September 2010.

238. ^ "Commemorating the Royal Visit by Ijahnya Christian", *The Anguillan Newspaper*, 22 April 2005.

239. ^ White, pp. 15, 210, 211.

240. ^ Bogues, Anthony (2003), *Black Heretics, Black Prophets: Radical Political Intellectuals*. Psychology Press. ISBN 0415943256, p. 189.

241. ^ Bradley, Lloyd (2001), *This Is Reggae Music: The Story of Jamaica's Music*. Grove Press. ISBN 0802138284, pp. 192–93.

242. ^ Jump up to:^{a b c} Edmonds, Ennis Barrington (2002), *Rastafari: From Outcasts to Culture Bearers*. Oxford University Press. ISBN 0198030606. p. 86.

243. ^ Jump up to:^{a b} Habekost, Christian (1993), *Verbal Riddim: The Politics and Aesthetics of African-Caribbean Dub Poetry*. Rodopi. ISBN 9051835493, p. 83.

244. ^ Jump up to:^{a b} O'Brien Chang, Kevin; Chen, Wayne (1998). *Reggae Routes: The Story of Jamaican Music*. Temple University Press. p. 243. ISBN 978-1-56639-629-5.

245. ^ "African Crossroads – Spiritual Kinsmen". Archived from the original on 15 January 2008. Retrieved 1 January 2008. Dr. Ikael Tafari, *The Daily Nation*, 24 December 2007.

246. ^ White, p. 211.

247. ^ Funk, Jerry (2007), *Life Is an Excellent Adventure*. Trafford Publishing. ISBN 1412215005, p. 149.

248. ^ Burke, Michael (1 March 2017). "PNP strategies in the 1972 campaign". *Jamaica Observer*.

249. ^ Norris, Gregory (13 October 2014). "Rod of Correction". *Addis Standard*.

250. ^ Marley, Rita (2004). *No Woman No Cry: My Life with Bob Marley*. Hyperion. p. 43. ISBN 978-0-7868-6867-4.

251. ^ "Bob Marley the Devoted Rastafarian!". Rasta-man-vibration.com. Retrieved 12 September 2010.

252. ^ Spencer, William David (1998). *Dread Jesus*. SPCK Publishing. p. 44. ISBN 978-0-28105101-4.

253. ^ Hood, Robert Earl (January 1990). *Must God Remain Greek?: Afro Cultures and God-talk*. Fortress Press. pp. 93–. ISBN 978-0-8006-2449-1.

254. ^ Crewe, Quentin (1987). *Touch the Happy Isles: A Journey through the Caribbean*. London: Michael Joseph Ltd. p. 286. ISBN 0718128222.

255. ^ "Archbishop Abuna Yesehaq Interview". YouTube. Archived from the original on 28 October 2021. Retrieved 2 January 2021.

256. ^ "Ethiopians in D.C. Region Mourn Archbishop's Death". The Washington Post. 13 January 2006.

257. ^ Workneh, Fikre Mariam (31 December 2018). "Abune Theophilus and Emperor Haile Selassie I: Their Invaluable Contributions to the Ethiopian Orthodox Church". ecadforum.com. ECADF. Archived from the original on 23 August 2020. Retrieved 2 January 2021.

258. ^ Funk, Jerry (2003). *Life Is an Excellent Adventure: An Irreverent Personal Odyssey*. Victoria, Canada: CreateSpace Independent Publishing Platform. pp. 148–150. ISBN 1412008484.

259. ^ "A Tale of Two Nations". ethiopianworldfederation.org. The Ethiopian World Federation Incorporated. Retrieved 14 March 2022.

260. ^ "The History and Location of the Shashamane Settlement Community Development Foundation, Inc., USA". Shashamane. Archived from the original on 25 May 2011. Retrieved 12 September 2010.

261. ^ Price, Charles. Review: Erin C. Macleod *Visions of Zion: Ethiopians and Rastafari in the Search for the Promised Land*. University of Chicago Press.
p. 223. doi:10.1086/683071. JSTOR 10.1086/683071. S2CID 162427664.

262. ^ Summers, Chris. "The Rastafarians' flawed African 'promised land'". BBC News.

263. ^ Gomes, Shelene (2018). "Counter-Narratives of Belonging: Rastafari in the Promised Land". The Global South. Indiana University Press. 12 (1): 115. doi:10.2979/globalsouth.12.1.07. JSTOR 10.2979/globalsouth.12.1.07. S2CID 164637705.

264. ^ Reston, James (13 July 1940). "BRITISH RECOGNIZE ETHIOPIA AS ALLY; Promise to Release Country From Italian Domination if the War Is Won BACK HAILE SELASSIE RULE Army Heads in East Africa Seek to Coordinate Efforts of Tribal Chiefs for Attack Reversal of 1938 Position 200,000 Ethiopian Fighters Ready". The New York Times.

265. ^ "Person of the Year". Time. 1935.

266. ^ "The Emperor returns to Addis Ababa". British Pathe. 1941.

267. ^ "EMPEROR HAILE SELASSIE I MEET THE PRESS INTERVIEW". 13 October 2016.

268. ^ Selassie, Haile; Cousins, Norman; Daniel, Clifton; Frederick, Pauline; Freudenheim, Milton; Spivak, Lawrence (1972). "Meet the press: Sunday, October 6, 1963 with guest His Imperial Majesty, Haile Selassie I, Emperor of Ethiopia". World Cat.

269. ^ "TV: A Question of Taste; N.B.C. Documentary Comes Close to Ridiculing Selassie's 1963 State Visit". The New York Times. 4 March 1964.

270. ^ Vestal, Theodore M. (2009). "The Lion of Judah at Camelot: U.S. Foreign Policy Towards Ethiopia as Reflected in the Second State Visit of Emperor Haile Selassie to the United States". International Journal of Ethiopian Studies. 4 (1/2): 135–152. JSTOR 27828908.

271. ^ David, Talbot (1955). Haile Selassie I: Silver Jubilee. Ethiopia: W.P. van Stockum. ISBN 9780-9-7936-1937.

272. ^ Keller, Edmond J. (2010). _"Constitutionalism, Citizenship and Political Transitions In Ethiopia: Historic and Contemporary Process"_ (PDF). UCLA World Press: 66–67.

273. ^ Bellucci, Stefano (18 September 2022). _"The 1974 Ethiopian Revolution at 40: Social, Economic, and Political Legacies"_. Northeast African Studies. 16 (1): 1–13. doi:10.14321/nortafristud.16.1.0001. S2CID 148384238.

274. ^ _"Haile Selassie I"_. South African History Online.

275. ^ _"The last emperor of Ethiopia: Haile Selassie's legacy remains divisive"_. France 24. 15 May 2020.

276. ^ _"Commemorating Haile Selassie's Pan-African Legacy"_. Ethiopian News Agency. 2019.

277. ^ _"Haile Selassie - Ethiopia's 'Lion of Judah'"_. Deutsche Welle. 15 June 2018. Archived from the original on 15 June 2018.

278. ^ Abel, Tesfaye (17 October 2016). _"Abel Tesfaye on X: "anbessa

Garter By Edward Bainbridge Copnall 1907-1973". Selling Antiques.

284. ^ "Mask of Ethiopian Emperor Haile Selassie by artists Beulah Woodward, Los Angeles, circa September 1935". September 1935.

285. ^ "Haile Selassie". Smithsonian American Art Museum.

286. ^ "Haile Selassie (1892-1975)".

287. ^ Jeffrey, James (18 October 2019). "Ethiopia opens its secretive Imperial Palace for first time". CNN.

288. ^ "African Union Unveils a Statue of Former Ethiopian Emperor Haile Selassie I". African Union. 10 February 2019.

289. ^ Getachew, Addis; Twessema, Seleshi (2 October 2019). "African leaders unveil statue of last Ethiopian emperor". Anadolu Agency.

290. ^ "Haile Selassie: Why the African Union put up a statue". BBC News. 10 February 2019. Archived from the original on 11 February 2019.

291. ^ "Haile Selassie Statue, AU Headquarters" (PDF). Contested Histories.

292. ^ Scourfield, Stephen (8 May 2014). "The legacy of Haile Selassie". The West Australian.

293. ^ "50th Anniversary Founders Day Celebration Haile Selassie High School (Jamaica)". Rita Marley Foundation. 28 April 2016.

294. ^ "Haile Selassie: Statue of former Ethiopian leader destroyed in London park". BBC News. 1 July 2020.

295. ^ Braddick, Imogen (2 July 2020). "Statue of former Ethiopian leader Haile Selassie destroyed 'by group of 100 people' in Wimbledon park". Evening Standard.

296. ^ "London Police Probe Destruction Of Haile Selassie Statue". *Agency France-Presse* via *Barrons*. 2 July 2020.

297. ^ Lenser, Loise (20 January 2024). "Nairobi Expressway Launches New Exit at Haile Selassie". *Box raft Limited*.

298. ^ Mbuthia, Bashir (20 January 2024). "Transport CS Murk omen To Launch Nairobi Expressway Haile Selassie Exit Plaza". *Citizen TV*.

299. ^ Vestal, Theodore M. (2011). *The Lion of Judah in the New World: Emperor Haile Selassie of Ethiopia and the Shaping of Americans' Attitudes Toward Africa*. United States: Praeger. p. 19. ISBN 9780313386206.

300. ^ Selassie, Haile I (1976). *My Life and Ethiopia's Progress: The Autobiography of Emperor Haile Selassie I, translated from Amharic by Edward Ullendorff*. Great Britain: Oxford University Press. p. 155. ISBN 0197135897.

301. ^ Selassie, Haile I (1976). *My Life and Ethiopia's Progress: The Autobiography of Emperor Haile Selassie I, translated from Amharic by Edward Ullendorff*. Great Britain: Oxford University Press. p. 172. ISBN 0197135897.

302. ^ McPartlin, Joan (29 May 1954). "Boston to Welcome Ruler of Ethiopia". *Boston Daily Globe*.

303. ^ ከበደ, በረሁን (21 September 1993). የአጼ ኃይለሥላሴ ታሪክ. *Addis Ababa*: አርቲስቲክ ማተሚያ ቤት. p. 903.

304. ^ Religious, Traditional & Ceremonial. *The Official Website of The Crown Council of Ethiopia*. The Crown Council of Ethiopia. Retrieved 13 August 2014.

305. ^ ከበደ, በረሁን (21 September 1993). የአጼ ኃይለሥላሴ ታሪክ. *Addis Ababa*: አርቲስቲክ ማተሚያ ቤት. p. 891.

306. ^ Religious, Traditional & Ceremonial. *The Official Website of The Crown Council of Ethiopia*.

The Crown Council of Ethiopia. Retrieved 2 January 2021.

307. ∧ ከበደ, በረሁን *(21 September 1993)*. የአፄ ኃይለሥላሴ ታሪክ. *Addis Ababa:* አርቲስቲክ ማተሚያ ቤት. *p. 893.*

308. ∧ ከበደ, በረሁን *(21 September 1993)*. የአፄ ኃይለሥላሴ ታሪክ. *Addis Ababa:* አርቲስቲክ ማተሚያ ቤት. *pp. 895–897.*

309. ∧ ከበደ, በረሁን *(21 September 1993)*. የአፄ ኃይለሥላሴ ታሪክ. *Addis Ababa:* አርቲስቲክ ማተሚያ ቤት. *p. 899.*

310. ∧ ከበደ, በረሁን *(21 September 1993)*. የአፄ ኃይለሥላሴ ታሪክ. *Addis Ababa:* አርቲስቲክ ማተሚያ ቤት. *p. 901.*

311. ∧ *"Mr. and Mrs"*. *Jet Magazine. VI(2): 23.* 20 May 1954. Retrieved 9 April 2021.

312. ∧ Copley, Gregory R. *Ethiopia Reaches Her Hand unto God: Imperial Ethiopia's Unique Symbols, Structures and Role in the Modern World.* Published by Defense & Foreign Affairs, part of the International Strategic Studies Association, 1998. ISBN 1892998009. p.119

313. ∧ Jump up to:[a][b][c] Ewing, William H.; Abdi, Beyene (1972). *Consolidated Laws of Ethiopia Vol. I. Addis Ababa: The Faculty of Law Haile Sellassie I University. p. 261.*

314. ∧ *"The London Gazette, Issue: 43567 Page: 1235. Retrieved op 17 January 2017".*

315. ∧ Copley, Gregory R. (1998). *Ethiopia Reaches Her Hand unto God: Imperial Ethiopia's Unique Symbols, Structures and Role in the Modern World. Defense & Foreign Affairs, part of the International Strategic Studies Association. p. 195. ISBN 1892998009.*

316. ∧ *"Ethiopia welcomes the Queen: Archive, 2 February 1965". TheGuardian.com. 2 February 2016.*

Sources[

- Marcus, Harold G. (1994). *A History of Ethiopia*. London: University of California Press. p. 316. ISBN 978-0-520-22479-7.
- Mockler, Anthony (2003). Haile Selassie's War. Signal Books. ISBN 978-1-90266953-3.
- Murrell, Nathaniel Samuel; Spencer, William David; McFarlane, Adrian Anthony (1998). *Chanting Down Babylon: The Rastafari Reader*. Temple University Press. ISBN 978-1-56639584-7.
- *Roberts, Andrew Dunlop* (1986). The Cambridge History of Africa: From 1905 to 1940. Vol. 7. Cambridge: Press Syndicate of the University of Cambridge. ISBN 978-0-52122505-2.
- Safire, William (1997), *Lend Me Your Ears: Great Speeches in History*, W.W. Norton, ISBN 978-0-39304005-0.
- Shinn, David Hamilton; Ofcansky, Thomas P. (2004). Historical Dictionary of Ethiopia. Scarecrow Press. ISBN 978-0-81086566-2.
- *"Distressed Negus"*. Time Magazine. 15 November 1937. Archived from *the original* on 24 May 2007. Retrieved 19 January 2010.
- De Waal, Alexander (1991). *Evil Days: Thirty Years of War and Famine in Ethiopia* (PDF). Human Rights Watch. ISBN 978-1-56432038-4.
- Selassie, Haile I (1999), *My Life and Ethiopia's Progress: The Autobiography of Emperor Haile Selassie I*, translated from Amharic by *Edward Ullendorff*, New York: Frontline Books, ISBN 978-0-948390-40-1.
- *White, Timothy*, ed. (2006). Catch a Fire: The Life of Bob Marley. Henry Holt & Co. ISBN 978-0-80508086-5.

Bibliography [edit]

- Harris, Brice; *Ullendorff, Edward* (February 1977), The Autobiography of Emperor Haile Sellassie I:

"My Life and Ethiopia's Progress, Oxford University Press, ISBN 9780-9-4839-0401

- Asserate, Asfa-Wossen (15 September 2015), King of Kings: The Triumph and Tragedy of Emperor Haile Selassie I of Ethiopia, Haus Publishing, ISBN 9781-9-1037-6645, JSTOR j.ctt1pd2ktb
- Coltri, Marzia A (March 2015), Beyond RastafarI: An historical and theological introduction, Peter Lang AG, Internationalis Verlag der Wissenschaften, ISBN 9783-0-3430-9592
- Selassie I, Haile (2000), Selected Speeches of His Imperial Majesty Haile Selassie I, 1918-1967, One Drop Books, ISBN 9781-5-0071-9432
- Yuajah, Empress (8 July 2016), Jah Rastafari : Rasta prayers & healing scriptures, CreateSpace Independent Publishing Platform, ISBN 9781-5-3337-9054
- River, Charles (16 May 2019), Haile Selassie : the life and legacy of the Ethiopian emperor revered as the Messiah by Rastafarians, Amazon Digital Services LLC - Kdp, ISBN 9781-0-9905-3887
- Yahudah, Abba (2 July 2014), A journey to the roots of Rastafari : the Essene Nazarite link, Trafford Publishing, ISBN 978-1-4907-3316-6
- Garvey, Marcus (2 May 2019), Emancipated From Mental Slavery, The Mhotep Corporation, ISBN 978-1-09-601330-3
- Jackson, John G. (2020), Ethiopia and the origin of civilization, B.N Publishing, ISBN 978-0-592-43884-9
- Pearce, Jeff (18 July 2017), Prevail : the inspiring story of Ethiopia's victory over Mussolini's invasion, 1935–1941, Skyhorse Publishing, ISBN 978-1-5107-1865-4

Further reading[edit]

- Nathaniel, Ras (2004), 50th Anniversary of His Imperial Majesty Emperor Haile Selassie I First Visit to the United States, Trafford Publishing, ISBN 978-1-412-03702-0ISBN 0-88229-342-7

- *Haile Selassie's war: the Italian-Ethiopian Campaign, 1935–1941*, 1984, <u>ISBN</u> <u>0-394-54222-3</u>
- *Haile Selassie, western education, and political revolution in Ethiopia*, 2006, <u>ISBN</u> <u>978-0-313-38620-6</u>
- *The Lion of Judah in the New World*, 2011, <u>ISBN</u> <u>978-1-910376-14-0</u>
- *Mosley, Leonard, Haile Selassie: The Conquering Lion. Prentice Hall 1965 LCCN 65-11882*

Wikimedia Commons has media related to *<u>Haile Selassie I</u>*.

<u>Wiki source</u> has original works by or about: *<u>Haile Selassie I</u>*

Wiki quote has quotations related to *<u>Haile Selassie</u>*.

- <u>Ethiopian Treasures – Emperor Haile Selassie I</u>
- <u>Imperial Crown Council of Ethiopia</u>
- <u>Speech to the League of Nations, June 1936</u> <u>Archived</u> 22 October 2015 at the <u>Wayback Machine</u> (full text)
- <u>Rare and Unseen: Haile Selassie</u> <u>Archived</u> 13 December 2011 at the <u>Wayback Machine</u> – slideshow by *<u>Life magazine</u>*
- <u>BBC article, memories of his personal servants</u>
- <u>Haile Selassie I Speaks -Text & Audio-</u>
- <u>Collection by Martin Rikli in 1935–1936, including photos of Haile Selassie</u>, open access through the <u>University of Florida Digital Collections</u>
- <u>The Emperor's Clothes</u>
- <u>A History of Ethiopia</u>

- Newspaper clippings about Haile Selassie in the 20th Century Press Archives of the ZBW
- *Grandpa Was an Emperor* at IMDb

Listen to this article (1 hour and 14 minutes)
Duration: 1 hour, 14 minutes and 0 seconds.1:14:00

This audio file was created from a revision of this article dated 20 January 2024, and does not reflect subsequent edits.
(Audio help · More spoken articles)

Haile Selassie		
House of Solomon		
Born: 23 July 1892 Died: 27 August 1975		
Regnal titles		
Preceded by **Zewditu I**	**Emperor of Ethiopia** 2 November 1930 – 12 September 1974	**Monarchy abolished**
Titles in pretence		
Loss of title Communist take-over	— TITULAR — *Emperor of Ethiopia* 12 September 1974 – 27 August 1975	Succeeded by **Crown Prince Amha Selassie**

show
- v
- t
- e

Emperors of Ethiopia (list)

show
- v
- t
- e

Chief ministers (1909–1943) / Prime ministers of Ethiopia (since 1943)

show

- v
- t
- e

Chairpersons of the Organisation of African Unity and the African Union

show

- v
- t
- e

Pan-Africanism

show

- v
- t
- e

Time **Persons of the Year**

show

- v
- t
- e

Rastafari

show

Authority control databases

Portals:

- 👑 **Monarchy**
- **Ethiopia**
- **Eritrea**
- ✝ **Christianity**
- **Somerset**
- **United Kingdom**
- **History**
- **Biography**
- **Politics**
- ⚖ **Law**
- ✛ **England**
- **Africa**

- Conservatism
- Liberalism

Categories:

- **Haile Selassie**
- **1892 births**
-
- **20th-century emperors of Ethiopia**
- **20th-century murdered monarchs**
- **20th-century regents**
- **1975 murders in Ethiopia**
- **Chairpersons of the African Union**
- **Christian messianism**
- **Burials at Holy Trinity Cathedral (Addis Ababa)**
- **Deified men**
- **Deified monarchs**
- **Ethiopian anti-communists**
- **Ethiopian Oriental Orthodox Christians**
- **Ethiopian Orthodox Christians**
- **Ethiopian pan-Africanists**
- **Ethiopian princes**
- **Governments in exile during World War II**
- **Leaders ousted by a coup**
- **Marshals of the air force**
- **Oriental Orthodox monarchs**
- **People from Addis Ababa**
- **Rastafari**
- **Foreign ministers of Ethiopia**
- **Solomonic dynasty**
- **World War II political leaders**
- **Heads of government who were later imprisoned**
- **Deaths by strangulation**
- **Chief Commanders of the Legion of Merit**
- **Chiefs of the Order of the Golden Heart of Kenya**
- **Dethroned monarchs**
- **Extra Knights Companion of the Garter**

- **Grand Commanders of the Order of the Federal Republic**
- **Grand Cordons of the Order of Valour**
- **Grand Cross of the Legion of Honour**
- **Grand Crosses of the Order of the Sun of Peru**
- **Grand Crosses of the Order of Christ (Portugal)**
- **Grand Crosses of the Order of Aviz**
- **Grand Crosses of the Order of Saint James of the Sword**
- **Grand Crosses Special Class of the Order of Merit of the Federal Republic of Germany**
- **Honorary Knights Grand Cross of the Order of St Michael and St George**
- **Honorary Knights Grand Cross of the Order of the Bath**
- **Honorary Knights Grand Cross of the Royal Victorian Order**
- **Knights Grand Cross of the Military Order of William**
- **Knights of the Order of Pope Pius IX**
- **Monarchs who abdicated**
- **People murdered in Ethiopia**
- **People of the Eritrean War of Independence**
- **People of the Second Italo-Ethiopian War**
- **People from Oromia Region**
- **Recipients of Hilal-i-Pakistan**
- **Recipients of the National Order of Vietnam**
- **Recipients of the Order of Merit for National Foundation**
- **Recipients of the Order of Polonia Restituta**
- **Recipients of the Order of Saints Maurice and Lazarus**
- **Recipients of the Order of the Liberator General San Martin**
- **Recipients of the Order of the Star of Ghana**
- **Recipients of the Order of the White Eagle (Poland)**
- **Time Person of the Year**
- **Unsolved deaths**
- **Controversies in Ethiopia**
- **Recipients of orders, decorations, and medals of Ethiopia**
- **Recipients of the Order of the Republic (Sudan)**